MY FIRST BRITANNICA

Africa

8

ENCYCLOPÆDIA
Britannica®

CHICAGO LONDON NEW DELHI PARIS SEOUL SYDNEY TAIPEI TOKYO

International Standard Book Number: 1-59339-048-3 (set)
International Standard Book Number: 1-59339-056-4 (volume 8)

My First Britannica:
Volume 8: Africa 2004

Britannica.com may be accessed on the Internet at http://www.britannica.com.

LAOIS COUNTY LIBRARY
3 0010 00806472 0

Africa

TABLE OF CONTENTS

Africa

INTRODUCTION

Who were the pharaohs?
What country was created as a home for freed slaves?
On what river would you find the Aswan High Dam? What was apartheid?

In Volume 8,
Africa,
you'll discover answers to these questions and many more. Through pictures, articles, and fun facts, you'll learn about the people, traditions, landscapes, and history that make up many of the countries and cities of Africa.

To help you on your journey, we've provided the following signposts in *Africa*:

■ **Subject Tabs**—The coloured box in the upper corner of each right-hand page will quickly tell you the article subject.

■ **Search Lights**—Try these mini-quizzes before and after you read the article and see how much - *and how quickly* - you can learn. You can even make this a game with a reading partner. (Answers are upside down at the bottom of one of the pages.)

■ **Did You Know?**—Check out these fun facts about the article subject. With these surprising 'factoids', you can entertain your friends, impress your teachers, and amaze your parents.

■ **Picture Captions**—Read the captions that go with the photos. They provide useful information about the article subject.

■ **Vocabulary**—New or difficult words are in **bold type**. You'll find them explained in the Glossary at the back of this volume. And there's a complete listing of all Glossary terms in the set in the ***Reference Guide and Index***, Volume 13.

■ **Learn More!**—Follow these pointers to related articles throughout the set.

■ **Maps**—You'll find lots of information in this volume's many maps.

■ The **Country Maps** point out national capitals. **Globes** beside Subject Tabs show where countries are located in the world.

■ The **Continent Maps** have a number key showing the location of all countries.

Cover photos (top): river running through Masai Mara National Reserve, Kenya, © Galen Rowell/Corbis; (centre): Zimbabwean pots for sale at market, Johannesburg, South Africa, © Neil Beer/Corbis; (bottom): Verreaux's sifaka, South Africa, © Martin Harvey—Gallo Images/Corbis

■ The **Icons** on the maps highlight major geographic features and climate. Here's a key to what the map icons mean:

- Deserts and Other Dry Areas
- Polar Regions and Other Frozen Areas
- Mountains
- Rainforests
- General Forests

■ The **Mini-Atlas**, found in Volume 13, offers detailed maps, useful data tables, and assorted photographs of each continent.

And don't forget: If you're not sure where to start, where you saw something before, or where to go next, the ***Reference Guide and Index*** (Volume 13) will point the way.

Verreaux's sifaka, South Africa

Have a great trip!

MY FIRST BRITANNICA

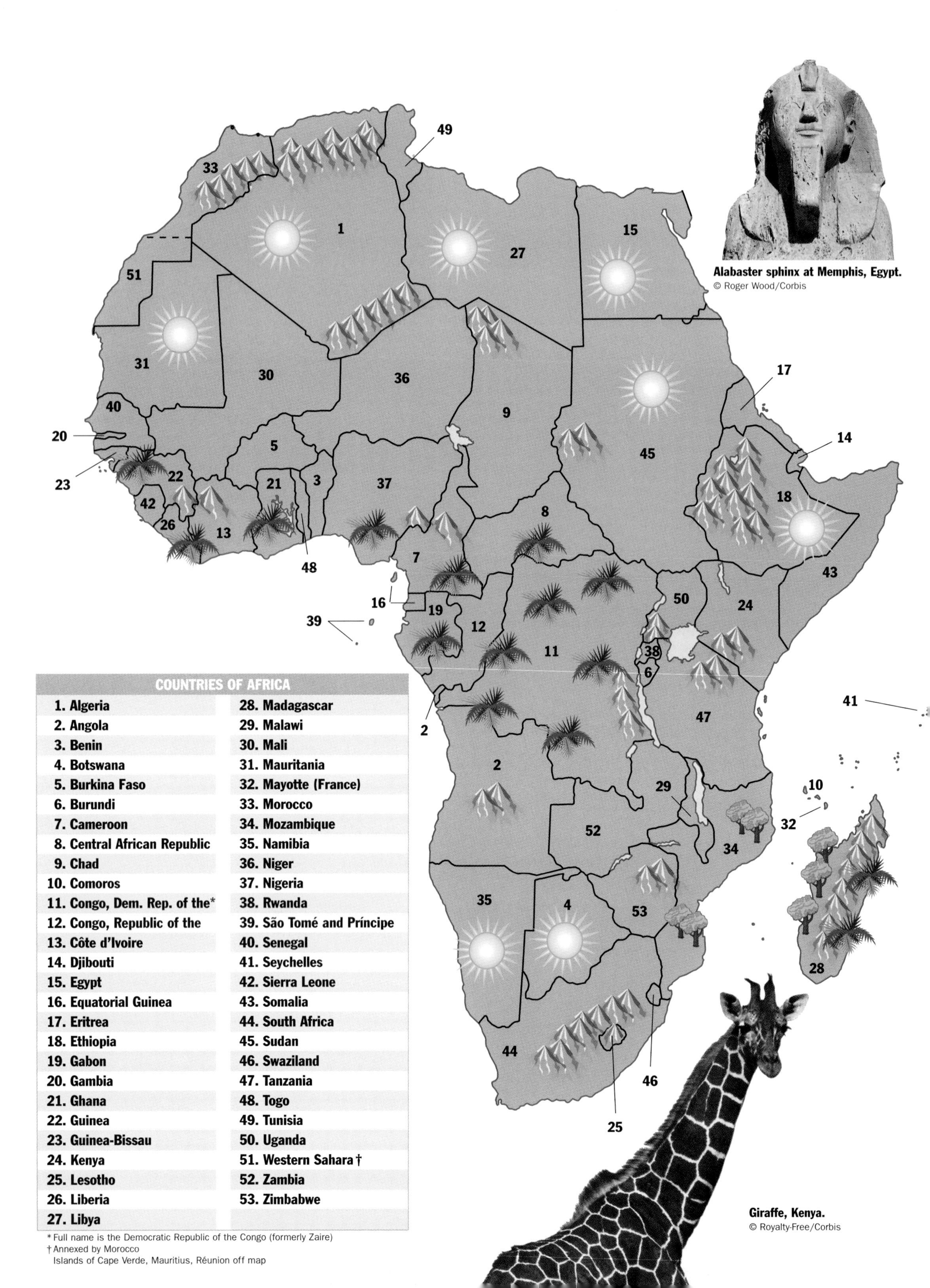

Alabaster sphinx at Memphis, Egypt.
© Roger Wood/Corbis

COUNTRIES OF AFRICA	
1. Algeria	28. Madagascar
2. Angola	29. Malawi
3. Benin	30. Mali
4. Botswana	31. Mauritania
5. Burkina Faso	32. Mayotte (France)
6. Burundi	33. Morocco
7. Cameroon	34. Mozambique
8. Central African Republic	35. Namibia
9. Chad	36. Niger
10. Comoros	37. Nigeria
11. Congo, Dem. Rep. of the*	38. Rwanda
12. Congo, Republic of the	39. São Tomé and Príncipe
13. Côte d'Ivoire	40. Senegal
14. Djibouti	41. Seychelles
15. Egypt	42. Sierra Leone
16. Equatorial Guinea	43. Somalia
17. Eritrea	44. South Africa
18. Ethiopia	45. Sudan
19. Gabon	46. Swaziland
20. Gambia	47. Tanzania
21. Ghana	48. Togo
22. Guinea	49. Tunisia
23. Guinea-Bissau	50. Uganda
24. Kenya	51. Western Sahara †
25. Lesotho	52. Zambia
26. Liberia	53. Zimbabwe
27. Libya	

* Full name is the Democratic Republic of the Congo (formerly Zaire)
† Annexed by Morocco
Islands of Cape Verde, Mauritius, Réunion off map

Giraffe, Kenya.
© Royalty-Free/Corbis

Land of Splendour

Africa's **splendour** is seen in its dramatic landscapes, its amazing animal life, and its **diverse** human culture. The African continent is the home of more than 800 million people living in more than 50 countries. Africa is the second largest continent on Earth, after Asia.

Africa's long coastline is shaped by the Atlantic and Indian oceans and the Mediterranean and Red seas. In the north of the continent lies the Sahara. It is the world's largest desert and covers almost all of northern Africa. Located in south-western Africa are two other major deserts, the Kalahari and the Namib.

The African continent has two major rivers, the Nile and the Congo. The Nile is the longest river in the world. At the southern end of the Nile is Lake Victoria, Africa's largest lake. Not far to the south-east of Lake Victoria is Mount Kilimanjaro, the highest point in Africa. One of the world's major waterfalls, Victoria Falls, is also in Africa.

Africa is known for its wildlife. There are elephants, rhinoceroses, hippopotamuses, lions, and leopards. Other animals include antelope, gazelles, giraffes, baboons, gorillas, hyenas, and chimpanzees. Most of these animals live in Africa's open grasslands or in tropical rainforests.

The people of Africa belong to hundreds of **ethnic** groups. Each group has its own language, traditions, religion, arts, and history. During its political history, Africa has been the site of Egyptian dynasties, African kingdoms, European colonies, and independent countries.

DID YOU KNOW?
Surprisingly, the coastline of Africa is shorter than the coastline of Europe, the second-smallest continent. This is because Africa has few inlets, large bays, or gulfs - features that add to coastal length by causing 'detours' away from a straight coastline.

SEARCH LIGHT

Find and correct the mistake in the following sentence: Africa is one of the smallest continents.

LEARN MORE! READ THESE ARTICLES…
ASIA (VOLUME 7) • CONTINENTS (VOLUME 1)
EUROPE (VOLUME 6)

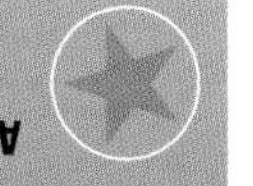

Answer: Africa is one of the largest continents.

SEARCH LIGHT

How did the Congo get its name?

Women gather firewood in the Democratic Republic of the Congo, which is also called Congo (Kinshasa). More than two-thirds of the people live in small towns and villages.
© Gallo Images/Corbis

DID YOU KNOW?

The Congo River is one of the great rivers of the world. Only the Amazon River (in South America) drains a larger area than the Congo River does.

Two Countries, One Name

Congo (Brazzaville).

Congo (Kinshasa).

As long as 25,000 years ago, people began to live in the forests of the Congo River **basin** in west-central Africa. They gathered food from the forests and dug up roots to eat.

Today the Congo basin contains two countries separated by the Congo River. Both of the countries are called Congo. To tell them apart, they are sometimes referred to by the names of their capital cities. One of the countries is called Congo (Brazzaville), and the other is Congo (Kinshasa). Congo (Brazzaville) is officially known as the Republic of the Congo. Congo (Kinshasa) is officially called the Democratic Republic of the Congo.

The Congo region got its name from the Kongo, or Bakongo, one of the main groups of people who live there. These people have been in the area for centuries, from the time when the Congo was ruled by various kingdoms.

The Portuguese arrived in the kingdom called Kongo in 1483. At first the newcomers were friendly to the people of the kingdom. By the 1530s, however, the Portuguese were sending the Kongolese away as slaves.

By the late 1800s other European countries had become interested in the Congo region. They valued the Congo River as a route for trade between the west coast of Africa and the interior part of the continent. The French and the Belgians took over different parts of the Congo. The local people didn't win their independence until 1960. Though free, each of the two Congos faced many problems. Both countries experienced periods of fierce internal fighting and struggles for power.

LEARN MORE! READ THESE ARTICLES…
AFRICA (VOLUME 8)
PORTUGAL (VOLUME 6)
RIVERS (VOLUME 1)

Answer: It was named for the Kongo, or Bakongo, people, who have lived there for centuries.

These miners work at the Ashanti gold mine in Obuasi, Ghana. Ghana has long been one of the world's leading producers of gold. Mining provides work for many of Ghana's people.
© Penny Tweedie/Corbis

SEARCH LIGHT

Why do you think people from so many other countries wanted to take over Ghana? (Hint: Think of Ghana's former name.)

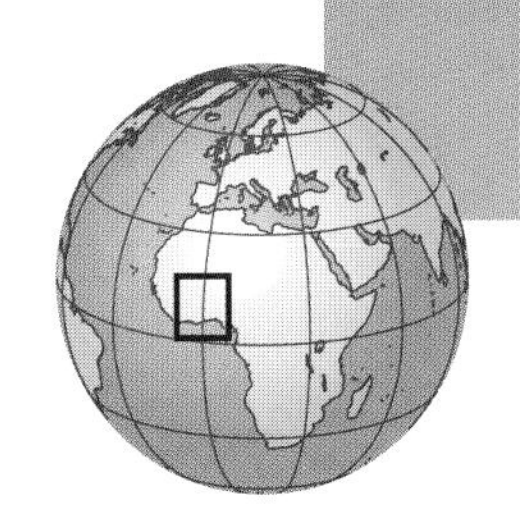

Gold Coast of Africa

The country of Ghana has so much gold that it was once called the Gold Coast of Africa. It still has the largest gold **reserves** in the world. Ghana is in western Africa. Accra is its capital and largest city.

Ghana has coastal plains in the south, **savanna** in the north, and hills and rainforests in between. The oddly shaped baobab tree grows in the savanna and coastal plains. There you will also find giant anthills, some of which are over 4 metres high. In the rainforests are tall trees such as the mahogany. And there are many kinds of animals - lions, leopards, elephants, buffalo, monkeys, and snakes, to name a few.

Many of Ghana's people work in fishing, logging, or gold mining. Farming is very important as well. Much of the farmland is used for growing cacao. These trees produce cocoa beans, which are used to make chocolate. Cacao, timber, and gold are sold to other countries.

Accra

Long ago the Almoravids from northern Africa conquered Ghana and forced its people to become slaves. Since then, many other groups have gone to Ghana. The Portuguese arrived in the 1400s. They traded in gold, ivory, and slaves. Later came the British, the French, the Dutch, the Swedes, and the Danes. In 1901 the British made the Gold Coast a **colony**. In 1957 the colony won its independence and became the new country of Ghana. Today Ghana is one of Africa's leading **democracies**.

LEARN MORE! READ THESE ARTICLES...
ACCRA, GHANA (VOLUME 8)
CACAO (VOLUME 10)
RAINFORESTS (VOLUME 1)

DID YOU KNOW?
Ghana's weavers are famous for their colourful kente cloth, which is made in narrow strips in beautiful patterns. The patterns have such names as 'thousand shields', 'the lion catcher', and 'gold dust'. The strips are sewn together to make clothing.

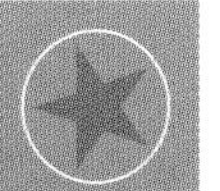

Answer: Ghana was called the Gold Coast for its vast reserves of gold. Throughout its history, many different people have wanted to control Ghana so that they could take its gold.

From Trading Post to Modern City

Accra is the capital of the West African country of Ghana. It lies on the coast of the Gulf of Guinea, which is part of the Atlantic Ocean. The city is built partly on a low cliff. The rest of it spreads northward across the Accra plains.

Accra reflects the cultures of the many people who have settled in the area where it now stands. The Ga people had villages there when the Portuguese arrived in 1482. The British, the Danes, and the Dutch came later. The Europeans built **fortified** trading posts along the coast. They traded in gold, ivory, and slaves. Because of the area's gold, it became known as the Gold Coast. In 1877 Accra became the capital of the British Gold Coast colony.

Children in Ghana enjoying a game called *mancala*, played with stones and cups.

The Gold Coast gained its independence from British rule in 1957 and took the name Ghana. Accra became the capital of the new country. Today it is a modern city of more than 1.5 million people.

Accra is Ghana's business and educational centre. The national museum and national **archives** and the Accra Central Library are located in the city. The University of Ghana is in nearby Legon. Black Star Square is the site of the Independence Arch. This large square is used for parades. For those who like sport, Accra has a football stadium and a racecourse. Not far from Accra are the Aburi **Botanical** Gardens, which were created by the British more than 100 years ago. And the city's large open markets receive most of the food supply each day.

LEARN MORE! READ THESE ARTICLES…
GHANA (VOLUME 8)
NIGERIA (VOLUME 8)
A STORY FROM GHANA: ANANSE AND THE WISDOM POT (VOLUME 5)

DID YOU KNOW?
Accra's name comes from *nkran*, a word in the language of the Akan people of Ghana. *Nkran* are black ants that are found all over the city and the surrounding area.

Accra lies along the Gold Coast, an area in southern Ghana that has rich deposits of gold. The Portuguese built this strong fort, now called Elmina Castle, in the Gold Coast in 1482. They wanted to keep all of the area's gold trade for themselves.

Answer: The British once ruled there. Part of the city is built on a cliff.

Forests and Minerals

Guinea is a country in western Africa on the Atlantic Ocean. Its capital city, Conakry, is a major port. Ships stop there to load up on Guinea's minerals and other products and transport them to markets around the world.

The land is divided into four main areas. A flat plain lies along the coast. Northern Guinea has open grasslands called savannahs. The grass there grows as high as three metres during the rainy season. To the east the Fouta Djallon **highlands** rise sharply from the plain. In the south-east is a hilly area with large forests. There are valuable teak, mahogany, and ebony trees in this area. But much of the forest is becoming open grassland because people have cut down many of the trees so that they can use the land for farming.

Most people in Guinea work as farmers, growing their own food. They grow rice, cassava, sweet potatoes, bananas, coffee, pineapples, peanuts, yams, and maize. Some crops are grown to sell to other countries. Guinea also has large amounts of such minerals as bauxite, iron ore, gold, and diamonds. These are mined and sold to other countries.

The people of Guinea belong to several different groups. In the Fouta Djallon region many people are Fulani. In northern Guinea are the Malinke. Other major groups in the country are the Susu, the Kissi, and the Kpelle. Until 1958 Guinea was a **colony** of France. Because of this the official language in Guinea is French. But many African languages are spoken there as well.

LEARN MORE! READ THESE ARTICLES...
AFRICA (VOLUME 8) • ATLANTIC OCEAN (VOLUME 1)
ROCKS AND MINERALS (VOLUME 1)

SEARCH LIGHT

True or false? Most of the people in Guinea work as miners.

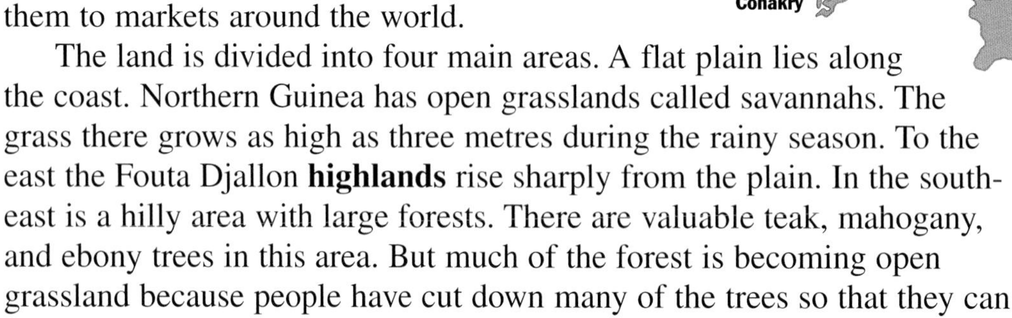

The savannahs of northern Guinea have some trees scattered among the grasses.
© David Reed/Panos Pictures

DID YOU KNOW?

All three of western Africa's major rivers begin in Guinea. The country's Fouta Djallon region is the source of the Niger, the Gambia, and the Senegal rivers.

Answer: FALSE. Most of the country's people are farmers.

Women try to catch fish in a small pond north of Monrovia, Liberia. Fish are a major source of protein for many Liberians.

DID YOU KNOW?
Liberia means 'land of the free', a fitting name for a country created for freed slaves.

Africa's Oldest Republic

In the 1820s some Americans who opposed slavery bought land in West Africa. They used it to create a new country for freed slaves, whose ancestors had been taken from Africa. This country was called Liberia. Its government was set up as a **republic** modelled on the United States government. Liberia is now the oldest republic in Africa. Despite the origins of the country, most of its citizens are not the descendants of former slaves.

Today you can find out about Liberia's past by visiting the Malima Gorblah Village and Besao Village. These villages preserve the country's old culture. They are like living museums of Liberia's past.

Liberia's climate is warm and humid all year and rainy from May to October. The country's forests and rolling hills are home to such wild animals as monkeys, chimpanzees, antelopes, elephants, crocodiles, and poisonous snakes. There are two rare animals found in Liberia. One is the pygmy hippopotamus, which looks like a baby hippo even when it is fully grown. The other is the manatee, a big seal-shaped **mammal** that lives in the water.

The rubber trees, coffee, and cocoa that grow in Liberia provide products that can be sold to other countries. Liberian farmers also grow rice, sugarcane, bananas, and yams. Liberia is rich in mineral resources. It is one of the world's leading producers of iron ore.

Liberia suffered through a **civil war** in the early 1990s. It made life dangerous and difficult for many people. The war officially ended in 1996, but some fighting has continued.

LEARN MORE! READ THESE ARTICLES...
MANATEES (VOLUME 12)
MONROVIA, LIBERIA (VOLUME 8)
RAINFORESTS (VOLUME 1)

Fill in the gap: Liberia is the oldest ________ in Africa.

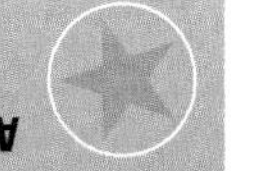

Answer: Liberia is the oldest republic in Africa.

DID YOU KNOW?

If you visit Monrovia, take your umbrella. Monrovia is the second wettest city in the world! It gets more than 5,000 millimetres of rain every year. Among the world's cities, only Buenaventura, Colombia, gets more rainfall.

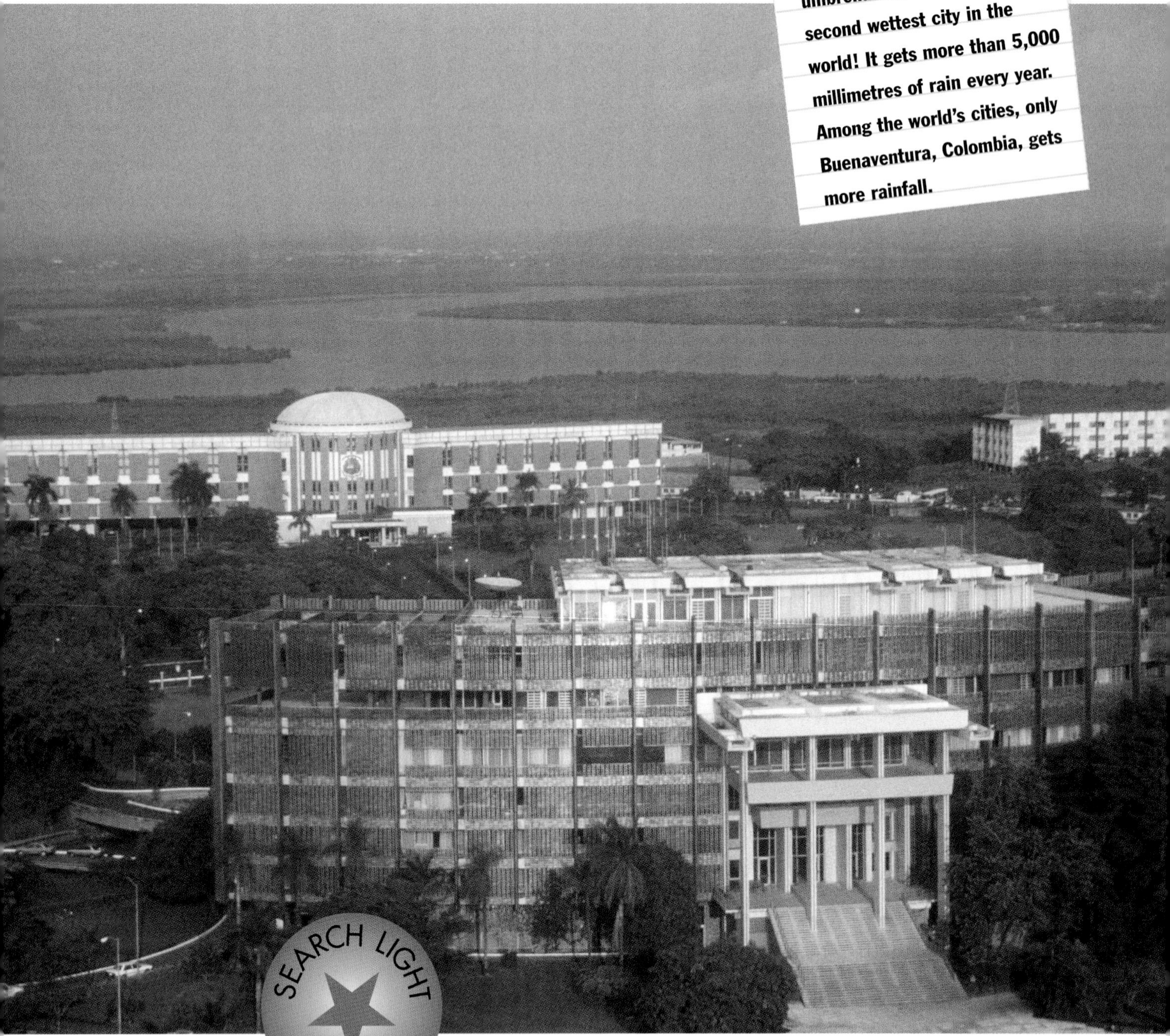

As the capital of Liberia, the city of Monrovia is home to the country's most important government buildings. The Executive Mansion (at the front of the photo) is where the president lives.

© Albrecht G. Schaefer/Corbis

SEARCH LIGHT

Where does the name Monrovia come from?

Freedom City

Monrovia is the capital of Liberia, a country in western Africa. It is also the largest city in the country. Monrovia is located on the coast, where the Mesurado River meets the Atlantic Ocean. It is Liberia's main **port**. Monrovia is not as old as many other cities, but its short history makes an interesting story of new beginnings.

A group known as the American Colonization Society founded the city. They set up a whole new country so that freed slaves from the United States could move to Africa, the home of their ancestors. Monrovia was named after the U.S. president James Monroe. He was the president at the time Liberia was founded.

Fishermen in Monrovia hauling in their nets.
© Eldad Rafaeli/Corbis

The first settlement was established in 1822. It later developed into the city of Monrovia. Liberia became an independent republic in 1847, with Monrovia as its capital. Most of the settlers from the United States arrived between 1830 and 1871. No longer enslaved, they were full of hope for making a fresh start at life. Many people who already lived in Africa also moved to Monrovia and to the other new towns in Liberia.

In 1851 the government of Liberia established a university in Monrovia. That school, now called the University of Liberia, also has a medical school. Today many students attend university in Monrovia.

A hospital in Monrovia is named after another U.S. president, John F. Kennedy. Other important buildings in the city are the capitol, city hall, and the Temple of Justice. But many of these buildings were damaged or destroyed during Liberia's **civil war**, which began in 1990. A truce was declared in 1996, but some fighting continued.

LEARN MORE! READ THESE ARTICLES...
ATLANTIC OCEAN (VOLUME 1) • LIBERIA (VOLUME 8) • SENEGAL (VOLUME 8)

Answer: Monrovia comes from the name of the U.S. president at the time Liberia was founded, President James Monroe.

Land of 500 Languages

Nigeria is a country on the west coast of Africa. It's a place of great variety, in both land and people. More people call Nigeria home than any other country on the continent. There are about 250 different groups of people living there. And they all have unique traditions, ways of life, and languages. More than 500 different languages are spoken in Nigeria. But English is the official language.

The weather is not the same in all parts of the country. Some areas get a lot of rain. Other areas are very dry. Because there are different kinds of weather in different parts of the country, there are many kinds of animals and plants. There are thick **rainforests** as well as **mangrove** and freshwater swamps. There is also open grassland called the 'savannah'. There are small trees all over the **vast** savannah.

DID YOU KNOW?

It is said that more twins are born in Nigeria than anywhere else in the world. Twins are so common that they usually get the same set of names. For example, the Yoruba people usually name their twins Taiwo and Kehinde.

Wase Rock rises sharply above the surrounding countryside near Wase, Nigeria. This part of the country consists of savannah, or open grassland, with scattered short trees.
© Bruce Paton/Panos Pictures

Once, camels, antelope, hyenas, lions, baboons, and giraffes lived in the savannah. Red river hogs, forest elephants, and chimpanzees lived in the rainforest. Animals found in both forest and savannah included leopards, monkeys, gorillas, and wild pigs. Today these animals generally are found only in special parks.

Nigeria has many cities. The capital of Nigeria used to be Lagos. But in 1991 the capital changed to Abuja. Lagos is a very large coastal city with many businesses. But Abuja is in the middle of the country, which makes it easier for people to travel there. Lagos was overcrowded, too, and Abuja had more open land for building.

LEARN MORE! READ THESE ARTICLES…
AFRICA (VOLUME 8)
A NIGERIAN FOLKTALE: THE MONKEY COURT (VOLUME 5)
WOLE SOYINKA (VOLUME 3)

SEARCH LIGHT

True or false? Nigeria is a very rainy country.

Answer: FALSE. Parts of the country do get a lot of rain, but parts of it are very dry.

The religion followed by most of the people of Senegal is
a) Islam.
b) Christianity.
c) Buddhism.

A Soninke mother and child stand in the doorway of a traditional-style mud house on a bank of the Senegal River. Like most of the other peoples in Senegal, the Soninke are Muslim.
© Margaret Courtney-Clarke/Corbis

Land of Teranga

Long ago there was a house packed with men and women. They were inspected and priced like animals. The weaker ones died, and the stronger ones were shipped to the Americas to work as slaves. This slave house was on Gorée Island, which lies off the coast of Senegal, in westernmost Africa. Exactly what went on there is not known for sure. But Senegal was at one time involved in selling Africans as slaves.

But that was long ago. Today Senegal's culture is known for its *teranga,* a spirit of warm welcome toward outsiders. *Teranga* means 'hospitality', or 'welcoming heart', in the language of the Wolof. Many different groups of people make up the Senegalese nation. The Wolof are one of the largest of Senegal's seven main **ethnic** groups.

Despite their different backgrounds, the people of Senegal tend to live in similar ways. Most of the people practice the religion of Islam. And most live in small villages in the countryside. Each village has a water source, a mosque (Islamic house of worship), and a public gathering place. France ruled Senegal until 1960. The different groups of Senegal speak several different African languages, but French is still widely used as a common language. This helps people from different groups talk to each other.

Senegal is one of the world's main producers of peanuts. The country has wide rivers and good soil. The light-coloured sandy soil in the north-western part of the country is especially good for growing peanuts. Dakar, the country's capital, is a major centre for the peanut trade.

DID YOU KNOW?
Léopold Senghor, the first president of independent Senegal, was also an important writer. He was a leading poet of a movement that celebrated African culture.

LEARN MORE! READ THESE ARTICLES…
DAKAR, SENEGAL (VOLUME 8) • ISLAM (VOLUME 5)
PEANUTS (VOLUME 10)

The small island of Gorée, near Dakar, served as an outpost for slave trading for some three hundred years. Slavery became illegal in Senegal in 1848, and the trading post closed. Today, tourists come to Gorée to visit several museums and the remains of old forts.

DID YOU KNOW?

Dakar is at the heart of Senegal's thriving music scene. One of the city's most famous musicians is Youssou N'Dour. His songs blend a wide range of styles, from traditional African music to Cuban rhythms, Western pop, jazz, and soul.

City of the Tamarind Tree

SEARCH LIGHT

Many of the city's streets and buildings have French names. Can you work out why?

Dakar is the capital city and business centre of Senegal. Its name comes from *dakhar*, a local name for the **tamarind** tree. The city lies on the west coast of Africa, close to the most westerly point on the continent.

The French founded Dakar when they built a fort on the site in 1857. Even earlier they had begun to establish trade in the area. Since then Dakar has been one of the chief seaports of western Africa. It has a fine harbour. Natural limestone cliffs protect the harbour from the force of the waves.

The French opened West Africa's first railway line in 1885. The railway connected Dakar with the nearby island city of Saint-Louis. This helped Dakar grow into a centre for the **export** of peanuts. The city now has an international airport too.

Flower merchants in Dakar.
© Wolfgang Kaehler/Corbis

If you visit Dakar, you might enjoy seeing the IFAN Museum in Dakar. It has a fine collection of art from Senegal and other African countries. On the nearby island of Gorée is the Slave House, built in 1786. Many thousands of slaves passed through it on their way to ships taking them away from Africa. The Slave House is now a museum where you can see the tiny cells where the slaves were kept. There are also several old forts, a women's museum, and a maritime museum (about ships). Gorée is a tiny island with only about 1,000 people. It has beaches and a high rocky area called Le Castel, which offers good views of the island and Dakar.

LEARN MORE! READ THESE ARTICLES…
LIBERIA (VOLUME 8) • PEANUTS (VOLUME 10) • SENEGAL (VOLUME 8)

Answer: The French founded Dakar in 1857. They gave French names to many places in the city. These names are still used today.

DID YOU KNOW?

In the early 1970s the remains of some of the bones of 'Lucy' were found in Ethiopia. Lucy is believed to be an early ancestor of humans who lived between 3 million and 4 million years ago.

SEARCH LIGHT

Find and correct the mistake in the following sentence. Ethiopia is a young country located in the Horn of Africa region of eastern Africa.

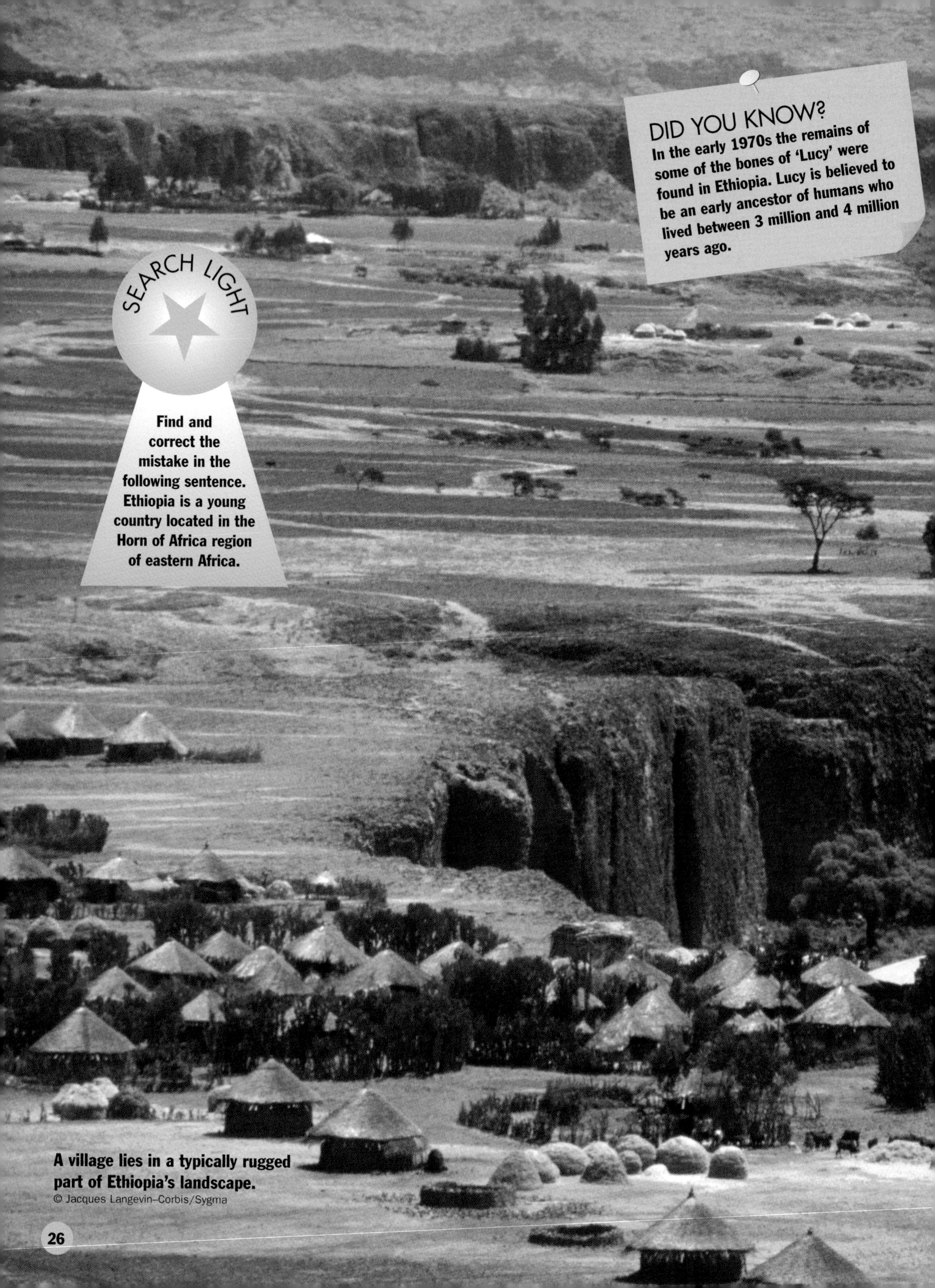

A village lies in a typically rugged part of Ethiopia's landscape.
© Jacques Langevin–Corbis/Sygma

Ancient Country in Africa s Horn

Not very long ago, a lot of people in Ethiopia, a country in eastern Africa, went hungry. In 1992-93 the Ethiopian government had to ask countries to donate food for its people. Some 10 million people faced starvation. Although many countries helped, hundreds of thousands of Ethiopians still suffered. Many later died because they had no food.

Most Ethiopians are farmers. But sometimes the government makes bad decisions on how to use the country's farmland. That's one reason why there's not always enough food to meet the needs of the people. Another reason is lack of rain. Ethiopia has two rainy seasons. But once in a while it suffers from droughts, times when it does not rain enough. Often Ethiopia must buy food from other countries. But Ethiopia sells things such as sugarcane, beeswax, leather goods, and coffee. Ethiopia is the place where coffee first came from.

Ethiopia is one of the oldest countries in Africa. It lies within a region that's called the Horn of Africa because on a map it looks like an animal's horn. The capital is Addis Ababa. Most of the people in Ethiopia are Christian. Some follow Islam. Others follow traditional animism, the belief that there is life in the forces of nature or even in **inanimate** objects.

One of the exciting things in Ethiopia is the rich variety of wildlife. But many of the animals have become rare, including lions, leopards, elephants, giraffes, rhinoceroses, and wild buffalo. In order to protect the remaining animals, the government has set aside 20 special parks and **sanctuaries**.

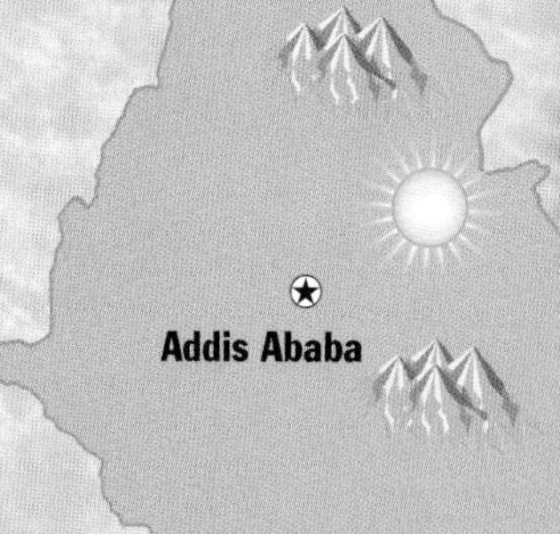

LEARN MORE! READ THESE ARTICLES…
ADDIS ABABA, ETHIOPIA (VOLUME 8)
CHRISTIANITY (VOLUME 5) • COFFEE (VOLUME 10)

Answer: Ethiopia is an ancient country located in the Horn of Africa region of eastern Africa.

DID YOU KNOW?
Many of the places in Addis Ababa don't have regular addresses. Many of the city's streets don't even have names. So if you go to Addis Ababa, be sure to get a guide.
SEARCH LIGHT
How did Addis Ababa get so many eucalyptus trees?

The City Called 'New Flower'

If you visit Ethiopia by plane, you will probably land in Addis Ababa. The city is the capital of Ethiopia and its largest city. Addis Ababa sits high in the mountains at an **elevation** of about 2,450 metres above sea level. It is the highest city in Africa.

At one time in Ethiopia's history, a town called Entoto was the capital. This town had a cold **climate** but lacked enough firewood to provide heat for the people. The wife of Emperor Menilek II wanted him to build a house at a nearby hot springs. The emperor did so, and a new city was founded around it in 1887. The emperor's wife named the new city Addis Ababa, which means 'New Flower'.

Wedding party, Addis Ababa.

As the population of Addis Ababa grew, that city experienced a shortage of firewood too. To help solve this problem, a large number of eucalyptus trees were imported from Australia. The eucalyptus trees eventually grew in number and now provide a forest for the city's needs.

Today Addis Ababa is the **headquarters** of several international organizations. One of them is the United Nations Economic Commission for Africa. Another one is the African Union. This league includes many African nations that work together to improve their economies and governments.

As a national capital, Addis Ababa has many of Ethiopia's government buildings. The city is also an important educational and commercial centre too. Addis Ababa University was started in 1950. And goods such as textiles, plastics, and wood products are **manufactured** in the city. Addis Ababa is also the site of one of Africa's largest open-air markets.

LEARN MORE! READ THESE ARTICLES...
ETHIOPIA (VOLUME 8) • EUCALYPTUS (VOLUME 10) • MOUNTAINS (VOLUME 1)

Merchants sell traditional textiles at an outdoor market in Addis Ababa.

Answer: The city had many of the trees brought over from Australia to provide a source of firewood. Over time, the trees grew in number.

Cradle of Humanity

Some of the very earliest humans are believed to have lived in Kenya. That is why some people call the country the 'cradle of humanity'.

Kenya is a country in East Africa. Its capital is Nairobi. The country has a beautiful natural landscape with great variety. There are sandy beaches, huge mountains, rolling grassland, and deserts. A long deep valley cuts through western Kenya. It is part of the Great Rift Valley, a very long series of cracks in the Earth's surface. It runs from south-western Asia through East Africa. Part of Kenya's south-eastern border lies along the Indian Ocean. Lake Victoria makes up part of Kenya's western borders. It's the largest lake in Africa.

Nairobi

The Kenyans are mostly farmers. In the Mount Elgon region, coffee and tea are grown and then sold to other countries. Mount Elgon is a volcano that no longer erupts. The soil in this volcanic region is especially good for growing crops. In the evergreen forests in the west are valuable trees such as cedar and podo. In the south of the country, most of the forests have been cut down.

Kenya's wildlife safaris are world famous. Many tourists visit the country to see the wide range of wild animals, including lions, leopards, elephants, giraffes, gazelles, baboons, and many others. In the rivers there are hippopotamuses, crocodiles, and many fish and spiny lobsters. Many of the animals that live in Kenya are very rare. The country has set up more than 50 national parks and preserves to protect its wildlife.

LEARN MORE! READ THESE ARTICLES…
COFFEE (VOLUME 10) • MOUNTAINS (VOLUME 1)
NAIROBI, KENYA (VOLUME 8)

SEARCH LIGHT

Find and correct the error in the following sentence: Kenyan farmers are mainly known for their rice and cabbage crops.

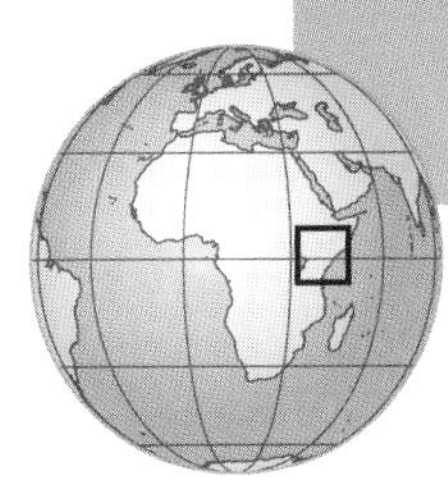

A group of Masai men perform a traditional dance in Kenya. All young Masai men are brought up to learn the group's customs. They are also encouraged to develop strength, courage, and endurance - traits for which the Masai warriors are noted throughout the world.

DID YOU KNOW?
Every year more than a million wildebeests, a kind of African antelope, pass through Kenya.

Answer: Kenyan farmers are mainly known for their coffee and tea crops.

DID YOU KNOW?
Nairobi is the largest city between Johannesburg, South Africa, in the far south of the continent, and Cairo, Egypt, in northern Africa.

From Swamp to Capital City

Nairobi used to be a swampy place. But this swamp would one day become the capital city of Kenya in East Africa. The name Nairobi comes from a water hole that the Masai people of Kenya called Enkare Nairobi. Enkare Nairobi means 'cold water'.

In the late 1890s, the British established a settlement there while building a railway across southern Kenya. This railway still runs through Nairobi. It connects Lake Victoria, on the border with Uganda, to Mombasa, Kenya's major **port** on the Indian Ocean. When the British took control of Kenya in 1905, Nairobi was made its capital city. Under British rule, Nairobi grew into a trading centre and a large city. It remained the capital when Kenya became free from the British in 1963.

A mosque in Nairobi.

Today Nairobi is an important centre for education. The University of Nairobi and its Kenyatta University College are among the major schools in the city. Visitors go to see the National Museum of Kenya, McMillan Memorial Library, and Kenya National Theatre. The **tourism** industry is important to the city's economy.

Just a few miles south of the city is Nairobi National Park. It's a large beautiful park set aside to protect the area's wild animals. It was the first such park established in Kenya. Tourists go to see the park's lions, black rhinoceroses, gazelles, giraffes, antelope, and zebras, as well as hundreds of kinds of birds. Near the main gate is a small zoo. Keepers there take care of baby elephants and black rhinoceroses.

LEARN MORE! READ THESE ARTICLES…
ENGLAND (VOLUME 6) • KENYA (VOLUME 8) • SWAMPS (VOLUME 1)

SEARCH LIGHT

Enkare Nairobi means
a) swampy place.
b) cold water.
c) hot city.

Once just a swamp, Nairobi is now a large city with modern buildings.

Answer: b) cold water.

SEARCH LIGHT

About how many islands make up the Republic of Seychelles?

The rocky islands of the Seychelles are rugged and beautiful.

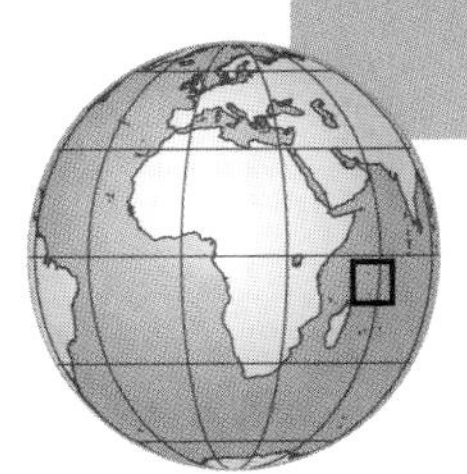

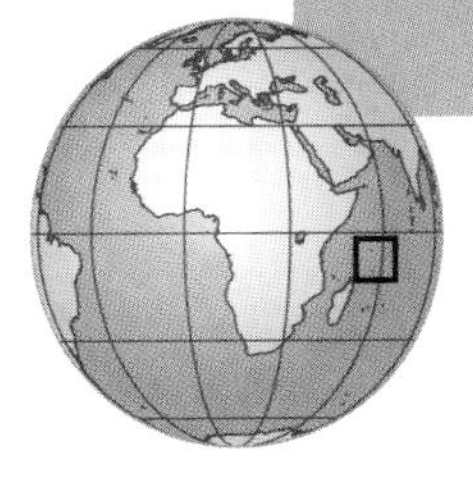

An Island Paradise

DID YOU KNOW?
The coco de mer, or double coconut tree, is found only in the Seychelles. Its nut can weigh almost 25 kilos and is the largest seed in the world.

The Republic of Seychelles is a country made up of about 115 islands in the Indian Ocean off the east coast of Africa. Victoria is its capital city and the only shipping port. It lies on Mahé, the country's largest island.

The Seychelles is made up of two main island groups. The Mahé group has 40 islands. These islands are rocky and hilly, with narrow strips of coastline. The other group consists of low islands built up from the rock-hard skeletons of countless coral animals. These coral islands have almost no water, and very few people live on them.

Mahé is home to the great majority of the country's people. Most of the people are Creole, with a mixture of Asian, African, and European heritage. The French and then the British used to rule the islands. The Seychelles was given its independence by Britain in 1976. Creole, English, and French are all national languages.

The islands have very little good farmland. Tree products such as coconuts and cinnamon bark are the main crops. Fishing is a very important industry. The people catch the fish, pack them into cans, and ship them around the world.

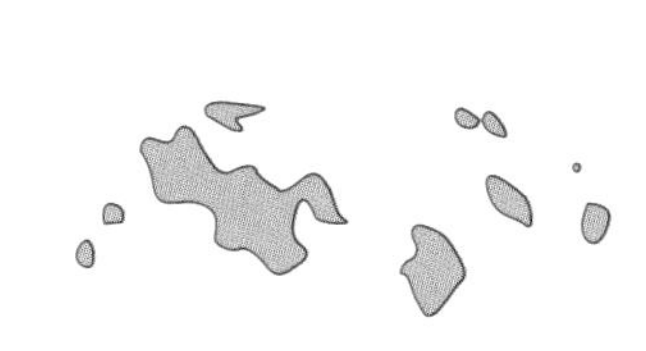

The islands are especially rich in beautiful **tropical** scenery. Coconut palm trees grow along the coast on most of the islands. Giant tortoises and green sea turtles live along the coasts. Sharks are found in the ocean. The seafaring frigate bird spends time on the islands. Tourism is the Seychelles' biggest industry, with visitors attracted by the country's beaches, wildlife, and greenery.

LEARN MORE! READ THESE ARTICLES…
CORAL (VOLUME 11) • ISLANDS (VOLUME 1) • PALM (VOLUME 10)

Answer: The country consists of about 115 islands.

Land of Nomads

Somalia is a country on the eastern coast of Africa. It occupies a region known as the Horn of Africa. It is called that because on a map it looks something like an animal's horn. The capital city is Mogadishu.

Mogadishu

Somalia has flatlands in the south and areas of rocky highlands in the north. It has a narrow sandy coast along the Gulf of Aden called the Guban. Most of the country is too hot and dry to have a great variety of plants. Forests exist only in the highlands. But in certain seasons there is rain. During the rainy seasons cars and lorries can get stuck in the mud. Because of this, camels, cattle, and donkeys are still used for transportation.

Somalia has many kinds of animals, including hyenas, foxes, leopards, lions, ostriches, and antelope. Such other animals as giraffes, zebras, hippopotamuses, rhinoceroses, and elephants have been hunted until they are almost **extinct**.

Many Somalis don't live in one place for the entire year. Instead, they move frequently to find grass for their animals to eat. People who regularly move around like this are called 'nomads'. For support and protection the people look to big family groups called clans. Most Somalis follow the religion of Islam.

Foreign powers, including England, Italy, and Ethiopia, controlled Somalia for a long time. Somalia became independent in 1960. But the country suffered through many wars, often involving fighting between different clans. Partly because of all the fighting, Somalia remained a poor country. The people have often faced hunger.

LEARN MORE! READ THESE ARTICLES…
CAMELS (VOLUME 12) • ISLAM (VOLUME 5)
MOGADISHU, SOMALIA (VOLUME 8)

SEARCH LIGHT

Most of Somalia is
a) hot and dry.
b) cold and dry.
c) cold and wet.

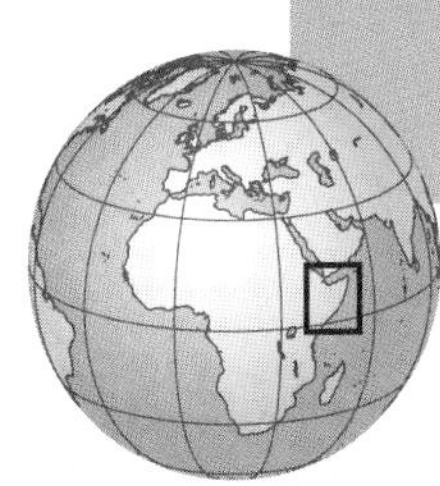

DID YOU KNOW?
Point Xaafuun, on Somalia's eastern coast, is the easternmost point in all of Africa.

Years of fighting in Somalia have left many of the country's people poor and hungry.
© David Turnley/Corbis

Answer: a) hot and dry.

Seaside Somalian Capital

Mogadishu is the capital of Somalia, a country in eastern Africa. The city lies along the Indian Ocean. Mogadishu is a major port. It is also the largest city in the country.

A big part of the city is in ruins today. It is hard to think that at one time Mogadishu was a lively city with bright whitewashed walls. There were beautiful **mosques** topped by tall towers called 'minarets'. But years of internal fighting in Somalia have left the city a ghost of its former self.

DID YOU KNOW?
Mogadishu's prominent location has made it a port of call for many travellers. In the early 15th century, the famous Chinese admiral Zheng He stopped there on three of his voyages throughout the Indian Ocean.

Arab settlers from the Persian Gulf set up the city in about the 10th century. The city traded goods with the Arab states, the Portuguese, and the leaders of Muscat (Oman) in the Middle East. The city's trade grew to include Persia, India, and China. During that time the city grew wealthy and powerful. In the 16th century, the Portuguese saw the success of the city and wanted to own it. But they were never able to take it over. In the late 19th century, Italy was in charge of the city.

In 1960 Mogadishu became the capital of Somalia. By that time Somalia was independent. Building began in the new city. The style of the old buildings and mosques mixed well with the style of the new ones.

But a **civil war** broke out in Somalia starting in the 1980s. Many people died during the fighting, and there was damage everywhere.

SEARCH LIGHT

Find and correct the mistake in the following sentence: Mogadishu, the capital of Somalia, is a young city.

LEARN MORE! READ THESE ARTICLES…
INDIAN OCEAN (VOLUME 1) • ITALY (VOLUME 6) • SOMALIA (VOLUME 8)

Mogadishu, SOMALIA

Schoolchildren listen to a lesson in a classroom in Mogadishu.

Answer: Mogadishu, the capital of Somalia, is an old city.

SEARCH LIGHT

Fill in the gaps: Almost half the world's population of ________ ________ are found in Uganda.

The source of the Nile River was a mystery that had fascinated people since ancient times. It wasn't until 1862 that explorers found out for sure that a major source of the river is Lake Victoria in Uganda. Here the river flows through the Source of the Nile Park.

DID YOU KNOW?

The gentle and friendly crested crane is the official bird of Uganda. This bird has feathers of red, yellow, and black - the same colours that are in the national flag. In fact, the crested crane is portrayed at the flag's centre.

Country of Lakes and Rivers

Uganda is a beautiful country in East Africa with many lakes and rivers, vast grasslands, and some forests. Most of the country lies on a **plateau** bordered by mountains and valleys. The capital city, Kampala, is built on seven hills.

Water is plentiful in Uganda. There are eight main rivers and six major lakes. Among the main rivers are two sections of the Nile River. Lake Victoria is the world's second largest freshwater lake. About half of it lies within Uganda. The area around this lake has some of the best soil in the world for growing crops. Most of the country receives plenty of rainfall too.

Uganda is home to many kinds of animals. There are hippopotamuses and crocodiles in most of the lakes and rivers. Zebras, giraffes, and antelope roam the grasslands. The country has developed several national parks to protect its animals. In these parks live lions, leopards, rhinoceroses, elephants, and chimpanzees. The Bwindi Impenetrable National Park contains nearly half the world's population of mountain gorillas, an **endangered species**.

At one time Uganda was a dangerous country to visit. In 1971 Idi Amin, an army officer, took power and became the country's **dictator**. The people welcomed him at first. But he was a cruel ruler, and the Ugandans suffered greatly. Amin started a war with Tanzania in 1978. The following year he was forced to leave the country. Afterward Uganda experienced yet more fighting, but peace eventually returned to the country.

LEARN MORE! READ THESE ARTICLES…
GORILLAS (VOLUME 12) • KAMPALA, UGANDA (VOLUME 8)
RIVERS (VOLUME 1)

Answer: Almost half the world's population of mountain gorillas are found in Uganda.

SEARCH LIGHT
Fill in the gap: Kampala is built on a series of ________.

City on the Hill of Antelopes

Kampala is the capital and largest city of Uganda, a country of East Africa. It lies in the southern part of the country, north of Lake Victoria. Kampala spreads over a number of hills. The rulers of the powerful Buganda kingdom of the 1800s kept antelope on the slopes. In the local language, Kampala means 'the hill of antelopes'.

Kibuli Mosque, Kampala.

Buganda came under the control of the British in the 1890s. The British chose Kampala as the site of their headquarters. For a while they controlled all of what is now Uganda from a fort on Old Kampala Hill. When Uganda gained independence from Great Britain in 1962, Kampala became the capital.

Kampala is Uganda's centre for business. It lies on **fertile** farmland and is the main market for the Lake Victoria region. Coffee, cotton, tea, tobacco, and sugar are sold there. And most of Uganda's large companies have their offices in the city.

Kampala serves as the religious centre for Uganda as well. Some well-known Christian churches in the city include the Namirembe Anglican **Cathedral** and Rubaga and St Peter's Roman Catholic cathedrals. Kampala's many **mosques** include the white Kibuli Mosque. It also has Hindu temples.

If you ever visit Kampala, make sure to go to the Uganda Museum. It has a collection of historical musical instruments that you can play. You'll also find a number of art galleries in the city. Northeast of Kampala, a place called Nyero is famous for a different kind of art. There you can see rock paintings that date back hundreds of years. No one knows for sure who made them.

DID YOU KNOW?

The Kasubi Tombs, on a hill overlooking Kampala, are the burial place of the kings of the Buganda kingdom.

LEARN MORE! READ THESE ARTICLES…
ENGLAND (VOLUME 6) • NAIROBI, KENYA (VOLUME 8) • UGANDA (VOLUME 8)

Ugandans shop for bananas at a market in Kampala. The city lies within Uganda's most important farming region.

Answer: Kampala is built on a series of hills.

Desert Land on the Sea

Algeria is a country on the north coast of Africa. It is the 2nd largest country in Africa and the 11th largest country in the world. The country's capital is Algiers.

Algiers

The northern part of Algeria is on the Mediterranean Sea. This area is known as the Tell. Two mountain ranges separate the coastal area in the north from the Sahara in the south. About four-fifths of Algeria's land lies within the Sahara, the largest desert in the world. Two huge sandy areas known as 'ergs' cover most of Algeria's desert. Not much grows on the desert's surface. But there are valuable minerals, **petroleum**, and gas underground.

Rainfall is very rare in the desert. At times, areas in the Sahara get no rain for years. There are also dry streambeds known as *wadi*s in the desert. If it rains, the *wadi*s quickly fill with water.

Most of Algeria's people live in the northern part of the country, where the climate is mild. That area receives enough water from rivers and rainfall to water the crops and provide people with water for drinking and industry. The people in Algeria are mostly Arabs, but many are Berbers. The ancestors of the Berbers lived in the area before the Arabs arrived.

Algeria was a French colony for more than 100 years. Hundreds of thousands of French people settled there. After a war against the French, the Algerians gained their independence in 1962. Most of the French then left the country.

LEARN MORE! READ THESE ARTICLES...
ALGIERS, ALGERIA (VOLUME 8) • DESERTS (VOLUME 1)
FRANCE (VOLUME 6)

SEARCH LIGHT

A *wadi* is a
a) northern part of the country.
b) dry streambed.
c) wide field of sand.

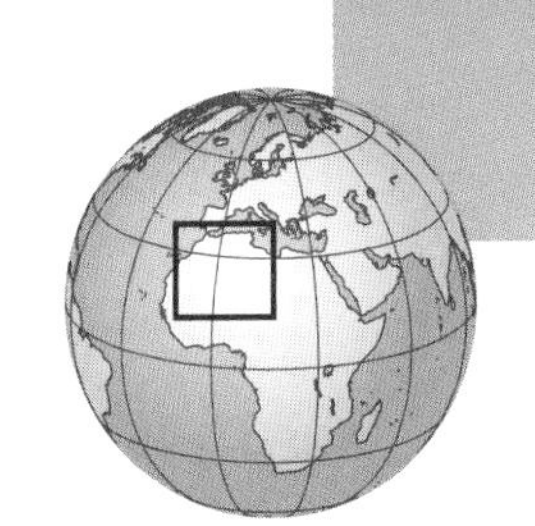

DID YOU KNOW?

The name Sahara comes from the Arabic word *sahra'*, which means 'desert'.

This trans-Saharan highway winds through the desert in Algeria. Historically, travelling through the Sahara was very slow and dangerous. But year by year modern roadways have been extended farther along the ancient trade routes into the desert.

Answer: b) dry streambed.

SEARCH LIGHT
Algiers is
located along
which body
of water?
a) the Algiers River
b) the Atlantic Ocean
c) the Bay of Algiers

The Island City on the Hills

Algiers is located along the **Bay** of Algiers in the North African country of Algeria. Much of it was built on the slopes of the Sahel Hills. From the harbour it looks like a large theatre with dazzling white buildings rising in steps.

The city has a long history. It was founded more than 2,000 years ago and has changed hands several times. In the 1500s the Ottoman Turkish Empire gained control, and the French captured the city in 1830. The French made Algiers a headquarters for a large territory they controlled in North and West Africa. The city became the capital of Algeria when the country gained independence from the French in 1962.

The city has two sections - one built when Ottoman Turkey controlled the country and the other built when the French ruled. The old Turkish city is on the upper slopes of the hills. It is full of high blank-walled houses standing on narrow winding streets. Much of it looks like it must have when it was first built. The most prominent building here is the fortress of the Casbah. This is where the last two Turkish governors of Algiers lived.

The French section of Algiers is built along the lower slopes of the hills closer to the harbour. This part of the city is full of big squares and wide streets. At the heart of the modern city centre are the University of Algiers, many foreign **embassies**, and a few skyscrapers. There are also the old palace of the archbishop and the Winter Palace, which used to be the home of the French governor-general.

DID YOU KNOW?

Algiers' name comes from the Arabic word *al-jaza'ir*, which means 'the islands'. This name may refer to the many small islands that used to be in the bay. Today most of those islands are connected to the mainland.

LEARN MORE! READ THESE ARTICLES…
ALGERIA (VOLUME 8) • ISLANDS (VOLUME 1) • RABAT, MOROCCO (VOLUME 8)

The old section of Algiers was built when the Ottoman Turks controlled the city hundreds of years ago. Along its narrow winding streets are homes, mosques, and marketplaces called 'bazaars'.
Collection Roger-Viollet/AFP

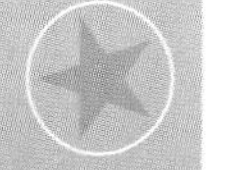
Answer: c) the Bay of Algiers

DID YOU KNOW?

More than 2 million blocks of stone had to be cut, transported, and assembled to create the Great Pyramid.

The Pharaohs and the Pyramids

Nearly 5,000 years ago there was a kingdom by the Nile River in a place called Egypt. The king was known as the pharaoh. People thought of him as a god.

The people of Egypt developed a great **civilization**. They built ships and sailed to other countries. They made great buildings. They carved and painted lovely pictures. And they developed a system of writing.

Three Egyptian kings - Khufu, his son Khafre, and his grandson Menkure - each ordered the people to build him a pyramid. The pyramids were to be the kings' **tombs**. A pyramid is a large structure with a square base and four sides shaped like triangles. The sides slope upward and meet in a point at the top.

SEARCH LIGHT

Fill in the gap: Three kings of Egypt ordered that giant _______ be built to use as their tombs.

After a king died, his body was carefully prepared and wrapped in many layers of cloth. (A body prepared in this way is called a 'mummy'.) Then it was placed in a splendid coffin that was placed in a room in the middle of the pyramid. The Egyptians believed in an afterlife. So they put all the pharaoh's treasures in the room too, for him to use in the afterlife. After that, the doors were sealed with stones.

The pyramids of the pharaohs can still be seen today. They stand by the Nile River near a town called Giza. The first pyramid to be built is perhaps the largest structure ever made by people. It is called the Great Pyramid. The other two pyramids stand beside it. It took thousands of workers many years to build the pyramids. But since the Egyptians had no heavy machinery, no one knows exactly how they were built.

LEARN MORE! READ THESE ARTICLES…
ARCHITECTURE (VOLUME 3) • CAIRO, EGYPT (VOLUME 8)
EGYPT: CULTURAL CENTER, PAST AND PRESENT (VOLUME 8)

In ancient times the pyramids built near Giza, Egypt, were counted among the Seven Wonders of the World.
© Larry Lee Photography/Corbis

Answer: Three kings of Egypt ordered that giant pyramids be built to use as their tombs.

DID YOU KNOW?

Many cities in the United States are named for ancient Egyptian cities. There's a Cairo in Illinois, a Memphis in Tennessee, and an Alexandria in Virginia.

The Aswan High Dam has allowed the people of Egypt to control the flooding of the Nile River for the first time in history. Now farmers can use the river's water for their crops year-round.

Cultural Centre, Past and Present

Egypt is a large country in north-eastern Africa. Its capital is Cairo. Most of Egypt is dry and rocky. But the Nile River, the longest river in the world, runs through it. In the north the Nile forms a **delta** before it flows into the Mediterranean Sea. The delta has Egypt's best farmland.

Because of the Nile and the water it brings, Egypt has one of the largest populations in the Middle East. People have lived there since ancient times. In fact, ancient Egypt was one of the world's earliest **civilizations**. The ancient Egyptians built large cities and many great monuments, including the pyramids of Giza.

Most Egyptians today speak
a) Arabic.
b) Aswan.
c) Coptic.

Almost 1,400 years ago, people from the Arabian Peninsula invaded Egypt. After that time, most of the people of Egypt began to speak Arabic. Most of them also accepted the religion of Islam. But a group called the Copts kept their native beliefs. The Copts belong to one of the oldest Christian churches in the world.

For much of Egypt's history, foreigners ruled it. Since 1952 Egyptians have governed themselves. One of Egypt's great achievements was the building of the Aswan High Dam on the Nile River. Egypt also controls the Suez Canal, a major transportation route. Egypt is considered a leader among the Arab states. And many of the greatest Arab writers and scholars are from there.

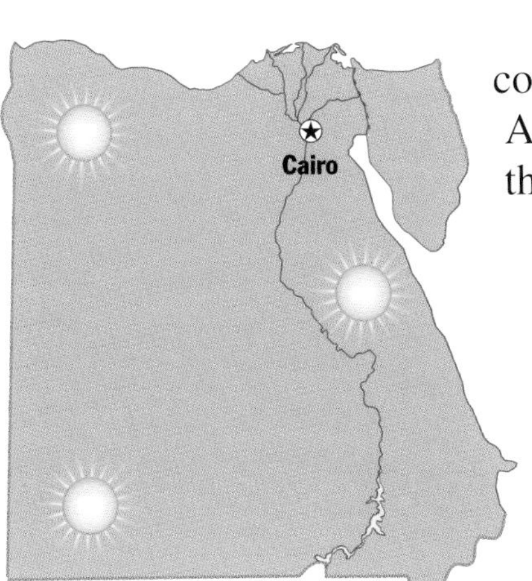

But Egypt has faced a number of problems. The country fought several wars with neighbouring Israel. And there has been a great deal of political violence by those wishing to change the government.

LEARN MORE! READ THESE ARTICLES…
CAIRO, EGYPT (VOLUME 8)
EGYPT: THE PHARAOHS AND THE PYRAMIDS (VOLUME 8)
RIVERS (VOLUME 1)

Answer: a) Arabic.

The minarets, or towers, of several mosques stand out in the 'City of the Dead' section of Cairo.

DID YOU KNOW?
The Arabic name for Cairo, Al-Qahirah, means 'the Victorious'.

SEARCH LIGHT
Find and correct the mistake in the following sentence: Cairo is the largest city in Asia.

City of the Nile

Cairo is the largest city in Africa. It is the capital of Egypt and is very old, dating back more than a thousand years. It stands on the banks of the Nile River.

Cairo has old and new sections. The old part of the city is very crowded. Most of Cairo's historic monuments are in this area. Along the eastern side of Cairo is the 'City of the Dead'. This area is the burial place of early religious leaders and **sultans**. But it's also home to hundreds of thousands of Egyptians who live in and around the tombs. Some of the new part of Cairo faces the Nile. It has broad streets with modern apartment buildings, skyscrapers, government buildings, theatres, and shops.

Cairo and the Nile River.
© Robert Holmes/Corbis

Shopping can be an exciting experience in Cairo. Khan al-Khalili is one of the world's oldest markets. It was set up more than 600 years ago. You'll find other markets selling things made of gold, silver, and copper. There are also places where you can get clothes, rugs, spices, and leather goods.

Cairo is known for its museums as well. The Egyptian Museum has the famous treasures of King Tutankhamen. The Museum of Islamic Art has many beautiful items made of wood, brass, and glass from different periods of Egypt's long history.

On the east side of Cairo are the Muqattam Hills. If you climb up there, you can look across the Nile to the Great Pyramids of Giza.

LEARN MORE! READ THESE ARTICLES…
EGYPT: CULTURAL CENTRE, PAST AND PRESENT (VOLUME 8) • RIVERS (VOLUME 1)
ANWAR EL-SADAT (VOLUME 4)

Answer: Cairo is the largest city in Africa.

Egypt's Gift

There's one country that depends almost entirely on the river that flows through it. That country is Egypt, and the river is the Nile.

Life would be **drastically** different in Egypt if there was no Nile. The river is the source of all the water used for farming in Egypt. That is why people call Egypt the 'gift of the Nile'.

People farm on the banks of the river. Two of the most important things they grow are rice and cotton. Egyptian cotton is one of the finest cottons in the world.

It rains very little in Egypt. Where it does, it's not much more than 17 centimetres a year. There are very dry deserts on both sides of the Nile. The plants you will find there are mostly thorny bushes and desert grass.

Long ago even Egypt's seasons depended on the river. There were just three seasons. *Akhet* was when the river was flooded. During *peret* the land could be seen after the flood. And *shomu* took place when the river's waters were low.

The Nile is **teeming** with different kinds of fish. The most common is the Nile perch. And the river is also an important waterway. Canals, or man-made streams, act as a highway **network** for small boats and ships during the flood season.

After its long journey across North Africa, the Nile empties into the Mediterranean Sea.

LEARN MORE! READ THESE ARTICLES…
AMAZON: THE RAINFOREST RIVER (VOLUME 9)
EGYPT: CULTURAL CENTRE, PAST AND PRESENT (VOLUME 8) • RIVERS (VOLUME 1)

SEARCH LIGHT

Which of the following descriptions matches the term *shomu*?
a) gift of the Nile
b) the flooding season
c) the low-water season
d) the season after the flood

DID YOU KNOW?

The Nile is the longest river on Earth. It flows through Uganda, The Sudan, and Egypt on its way from Lake Victoria to the Mediterranean Sea.

Answer: c) the low-water season

Joining Two Seas for a Shortcut

The Suez Canal is one of the most important waterways that people have ever made. The **canal** is located in Egypt. It joins the Mediterranean Sea and the Red Sea and separates the continents of Africa and Asia. It offers the shortest route for ships sailing between Europe and the lands on the Indian and western Pacific oceans, such as Australia and large parts of Asia. Before the canal was built, ships travelling between these parts of the world had to sail all the way around Africa.

Beginning about 3,900 years ago, people dug several canals roughly in the area of the Suez Canal. But none of them joined the Mediterranean and Red seas directly. The Suez Canal was created by joining a series of lakes across the **Isthmus** of Suez to form one long water passage between the two seas.

Watching a ship pass through the Suez Canal.

The Suez Canal has eight major bends. In some places it has been widened to form double channels called 'bypasses'. These allow ships travelling in opposite directions to pass each other. In the canal ships travel in groups and follow rules to prevent accidents. Each ship moves at a set speed, leaving a fixed gap between it and the next ship in the group. This keeps the ships from knocking against each other. A tugboat follows each large ship. The entire trip takes between 12 and 18 hours.

On average, 50 ships cross through the Suez Canal each day. Nearly 20,000 trips are made in a year. Most of the vessels using the canal are small tankers and cargo ships, though some passenger liners and warships also use the waterway.

LEARN MORE! READ THESE ARTICLES…
EGYPT: CULTURAL CENTRE, PAST AND PRESENT (VOLUME 8)
MEDITERRANEAN SEA (VOLUME 1)
PANAMA CANAL, PANAMA (VOLUME 9)

SEARCH LIGHT

Fill in the gaps: The Suez Canal joins the _______ Sea with the _______ Sea.

DID YOU KNOW?

By taking the Suez Canal shortcut, a ship travelling from London, England, to Bombay, India, cuts more than 8,000 kilometres off its trip.

Cargo ships like this one make up a large part of the traffic in the Suez Canal.
Hubertus Kauns/Superstock

Answer: The Suez Canal joins the Mediterranean Sea with the Red Sea.

Oil Country of Africa

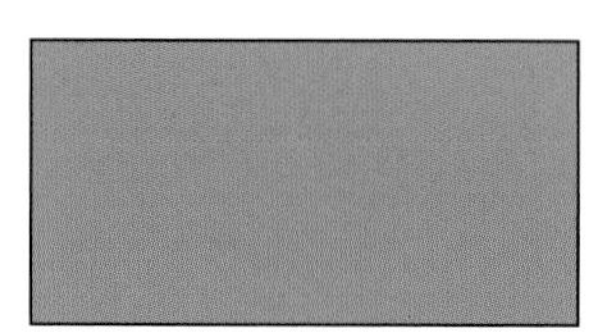

Libya was once a poor country. Then in 1959 oil was discovered in the desert. This made Libya one of the richest countries in North Africa. Some of the largest **petroleum** deposits in the world are in Libya. The capital city of Libya is Tripoli. It is located on the coast of the Mediterranean Sea and is one of Libya's major ports.

Libya has three main regions: the Sahara, Tripolitania, and Cyrenaica. The largest is the desert land of the Sahara, which is one of the driest places on Earth. There are very few plants in the Sahara. However, date palms grow in the oases, such as that found around the town of Sabha. An oasis is a **fertile** place in the desert where water can be found. Most Libyans live in Tripolitania, in the north-west. Many of the people keep sheep and goats. They also grow barley, wheat, tobacco, dates, figs, grapes, and olives. In Cyrenaica, in the north-east, the Akhdar Mountains and some oases are the main features.

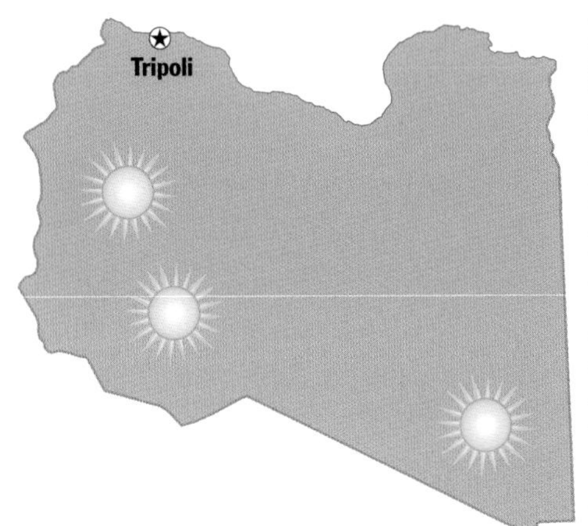

Many people in Libya identify themselves with traditional tribes, or *qabilah*s. The Berbers, the original people of Libya, were mostly coastal farmers. Today, however, most Libyans have a mixed Berber and Arabic **heritage**.

Libya became an independent country in 1951. It was ruled by a king until 1969. In that year a group of army officers led by Muammar al-Qaddafi took control of the country. Many people outside Libya have criticized Qaddafi for supporting terrorists and using his army to attack other countries.

LEARN MORE! READ THESE ARTICLES…
DESERTS (VOLUME 1) • OASIS (VOLUME 1) • TRIPOLI, LIBYA (VOLUME 8)

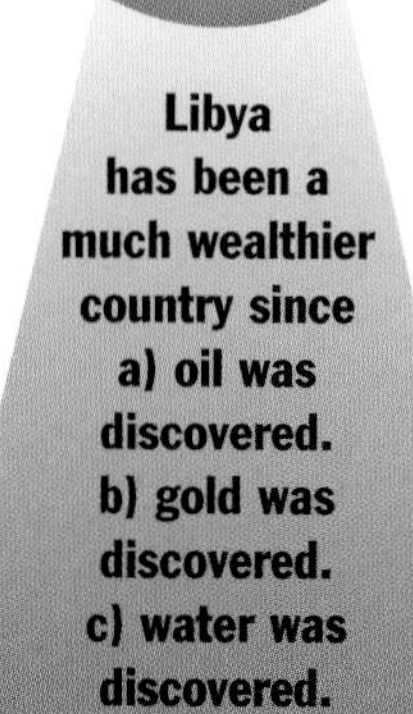

Libya has been a much wealthier country since
a) oil was discovered.
b) gold was discovered.
c) water was discovered.

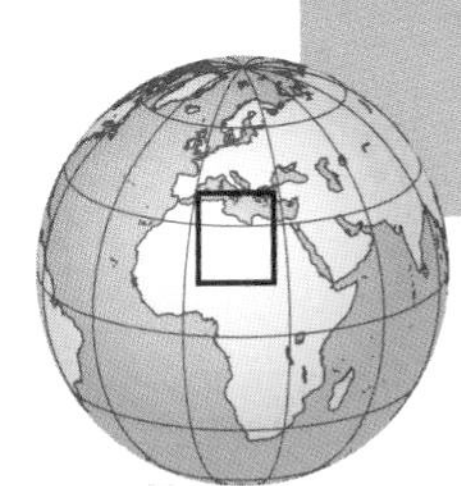

DID YOU KNOW?

The highest temperature ever recorded on Earth was measured at Al-Aziziyah, Libya. One day in September 1922, the temperature soared to 58°C.

A lake lined with palm trees forms an oasis in the Libyan desert.
Doug McKinlay/Lonely Planet Images

Answer: a) oil was discovered.

A wide street lined with palms leads into the city of Tripoli.
© Jean-Marc Charles—Corbis/Sygma

SEARCH LIGHT

Which answer below lists some of the peoples who occupied Tripoli in order from earliest to most recent?
a) Phoenicians, Romans, Arabs, Turks
b) Romans, Spanish, English, Turks
c) Turks, Romans, Phoenicians, Spanish

Ancient Walled City

Libya's capital city is Tripoli. It lies along the coast of the Mediterranean Sea in North Africa. It is the nation's largest city and chief seaport.

In ancient times the city was called Oea. It was one of three cities in the region that were founded by the Phoenicians more than 2,500 years ago. The other two cities were Sabratha and Leptis Magna. The cities were later ruled by the Romans, who called them Tripolitania (which means 'three cities'). Walls were built around each of the three cities to protect them from attackers. These high walls survived many invasions. Eventually, the walls of Sabratha and Leptis Magna were destroyed by invading armies. Tripoli grew more important as a result.

Playing football (soccer) in front of the former royal palace in downtown Tripoli.
AP/Wide World

In the 7th century, Arab Muslims captured Tripoli. They added a wall on the seawards side of the city. Three huge gates were built into the old wall for entering the town.

The ancient walls of Tripoli are still standing. But the city spread beyond the old walls long ago. Today the walled part of the city is called the old quarter or the medina. The modern city lies outside the walls.

The medina has narrow streets and is known for its **bazaars**. It also has a number of historic **mosques**. Many of these mosques date from the long period of Turkish rule, from 1551 to 1911. The most prominent structure is the Red Castle, a huge Spanish-style castle from the 1500s. Today it contains a museum about the city's history. From the castle one also gets an excellent view of the whole city, old and new.

DID YOU KNOW?
Football (soccer) is very popular in Libya. In 2002 Tripoli hosted the Italian Supercup. It was only the second time that the competition had been held outside Italy.

LEARN MORE! READ THESE ARTICLES...
ISLAM (VOLUME 5) • LIBYA (VOLUME 8)
ROME, ITALY (VOLUME 6)

Answer: a) Phoenicians, Romans, Arabs, Turks

Built for Victory

Rabat is the capital city of Morocco, a country in North Africa. It is located on the coast of the Atlantic Ocean. Modern Rabat has a rich mixture of cultures reflecting African, Arab, Islamic, and French influences.

Rabat has ancient roots. The city started out almost 900 years ago as a camp for Muslims who wanted to sail across the sea to fight in Spain. Later, the camp was named Ribat al-Fath, which means 'camp of victory'. A wall was built to protect the camp. Within the wall the city of Rabat began to grow.

Large parts of the old wall are still standing. Within them are the old town and the Jewish quarter. The Oudia Gate and the Tower of Hassan also stand as impressive monuments of the past.

France and Spain each controlled sections of Morocco for part of the 20th century. The country gained its independence in 1956. Rabat now houses government offices, universities, and art schools. The king of Morocco lives in Rabat for part of the year.

It's a short ride by road or rail to Casablanca, which is Morocco's largest city and its chief port. Like Rabat, it was once a base for pirates who attacked European ships. The Portuguese put a stop to the piracy in 1468. They later built a new town in the area called Casa Branca. The French called it Maison Blanche, and the Spanish called it Casablanca. All these names mean the same thing: 'white house'.

SEARCH LIGHT

What ruler lives in the city of Rabat today?

LEARN MORE! READ THESE ARTICLES…

FRANCE (VOLUME 6) • ISLAM (VOLUME 5) • TRIPOLI, LIBYA (VOLUME 8)

DID YOU KNOW?

The name Rabat comes from the Arabic word *ribat*. That word is often translated as 'camp' but can also mean 'monastery'. In North Africa it refers to a place were Muslim soldiers would gather either to study or to prepare for holy war.

A wall built hundreds of years ago still surrounds part of the city of Rabat.

© Nik Wheeler/Corbis

Answer: The king of Morocco lives in Rabat for part of the year.

DID YOU KNOW?

The name 'Sudan' comes from the Arabic term *bilad al-sudan*, which means 'land of the blacks'. This term was once used to describe all settled African lands south of the Sahara (a large desert in northern Africa).

Sudanese men rest on a wall near their camels, which are considered a symbol of wealth. Many people in The Sudan raise camels for their milk and meat as well as for transportation.

Giant of Africa

The largest country in Africa is The Sudan. It is the tenth largest country in the world. The Sudan is located in north-eastern Africa. Khartoum is the capital city. It sits at the point where the Blue Nile and White Nile rivers join together to form the mighty Nile River. The Sudan is one of the hottest places in the world. In Khartoum temperatures higher than 38°C may be recorded during any month of the year.

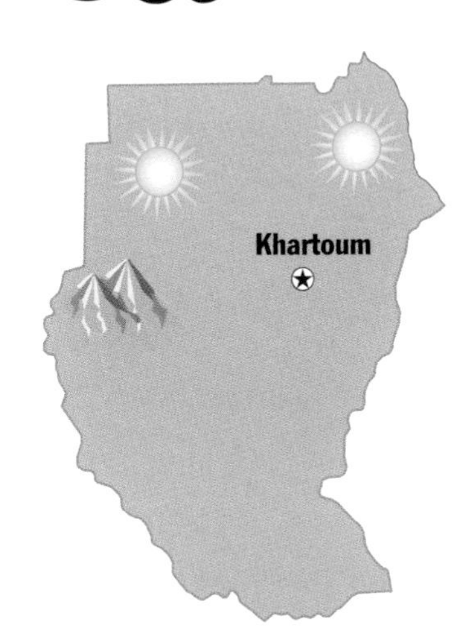

There are 19 major **ethnic** groups in The Sudan. More than 100 languages and **dialects** are spoken in the country. Many of the people either farm or rear camels and cattle. Roughly 10 per cent of the people live as **nomads**. Amongst all groups poetry and song are respected art forms. Both often reflect the country's mixed Arab and African **heritage**.

In 1956 The Sudan gained its independence from the United Kingdom. But fighting broke out almost immediately. The people living in southern Sudan opposed the new government, which was controlled by northerners. The southerners are typically black Africans who practise traditional African religions or Christianity. The northerners are typically of mixed ethnic origins. They speak a version of Arabic and practise Islam. The fighting continued until 1972, when the southerners were given control of their local government. But war broke out again in 1983. In 2002 the two sides agreed to stop the war, but fighting continued in some parts of the country.

SEARCH LIGHT

Fill in the gaps: Fighting in The Sudan has been mainly between people living in the ____ and people living in the _____.

LEARN MORE! READ THESE ARTICLES...
CAMEL (VOLUME 12) • NILE RIVER (VOLUME 8) • SAND (VOLUME 1)

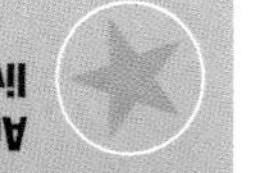

Answer: Fighting in The Sudan has been mainly between people living in the north and people living in the south.

An Angolan woman wears traditional dress.
Giacomo Pirozzi/Panos Pictures

SEARCH LIGHT

How were the Portuguese able to take control of Angola and stay in power there? (Hint: What would the Portuguese have brought with them to fight with?)

Land of Oil and Diamonds

Angola is a large country on the south-western coast of Africa. The Atlantic Ocean is its western boundary. Four countries shape its borders on land. Its capital is Luanda, a large city on the coast.

Most of Angola is a high **plateau** covered by savannahs, which are open grasslands with scattered trees. Roaming this land are leopards, lions, hyenas, elephants, and hippopotamuses. You may also see giraffes, zebras, and monkeys. With such rich wildlife, Angola has many national parks and nature **reserves**. However, some of the animals are in danger of disappearing because of hunting and other reasons. These animals include elephants, gorillas, chimpanzees, and black rhinoceroses.

The two largest groups of people in Angola are the Ovimbundu and the Mbundu. These two groups, and others, speak different languages that together are called Bantu languages. Almost all of the people also speak Portuguese, the country's official language.

Angola has many natural resources. Two of them - oil and diamonds - are major parts of the country's **economy**. Angola sells these products to other countries. But more people work in farming than in any other job. They grow **cassava**, maize, sugarcane, bananas, and coffee. In the south-west they rear cattle.

Portuguese explorers reached Angola in 1483. Over time, the Portuguese developed a **colony**. They ruled for almost 500 years. During much of this time, the Portuguese sent millions of Africans away from the colony to work as slaves. After years of fighting the Portuguese, Angola finally won its independence in 1975. But afterward the country struggled off and on with fighting inside its borders.

DID YOU KNOW?
Angola is rich in tropical woods such as mahogany, rosewood, and black ebony. These woods are used to make fine furniture.

Luanda

LEARN MORE! READ THESE ARTICLES…
DIAMONDS (VOLUME 1) • LUANDA, ANGOLA (VOLUME 8)
PORTUGAL (VOLUME 6)

Answer: In the 15th century, when Portugal conquered Angola, the Bantu-speaking peoples didn't have guns or cannons. The Portuguese had both.

A Portuguese Legacy

Luanda was founded by Paulo Dias de Novais in what year?
a) 1576
b) 1955
c) 1975

Luanda is the capital of Angola, a country in southwestern Africa. Luanda is in the northern part of Angola. It is the country's largest city. Located near the Atlantic Ocean, Luanda is a busy **seaport**.

Luanda was set up in 1576 by Paulo Dias de Novais from Portugal. The king of Portugal sent him to take over African land. Portugal ruled Angola for hundreds of years. Slaves were sent by boat to the Americas from Luanda. Angola finally became independent from Portugal in 1975.

Petroleum was found in the area in 1955. The Angolans sell this petroleum to other countries. This brings money to the city. Because of this, Luanda now has modern skyscrapers and wide streets. But there was a war in Angola from the middle of the 1970s until 2002. This caused a lot of **poverty** and other problems in the city.

If you visit the city, you'll be able to see the old fortress of São Miguel. You will also see the city's many churches. The churches are a **legacy** of Luanda's Portuguese past. There is also a museum of slavery in the city. Luanda has plenty of supermarkets, shops, and open-air markets. Roque Santeiro is always open and is one of the largest markets in all of Africa. You can buy almost anything there.

LEARN MORE! READ THESE ARTICLES...
ANGOLA (VOLUME 8) • OIL (VOLUME 2) • PORTUGAL (VOLUME 6)

DID YOU KNOW?

Luanda is one of the oldest cities in its part of Africa. Before the Portuguese founded it more than 400 years ago, the local people called the area Loanda. This means 'flat land'.

Luanda is a modern city with a busy seaport.
© Adil Bradlow—Trace Images/The Image Works

Answer: a) 1576

SEARCH LIGHT
Why did
Botswana
become one
of Africa's
wealthiest countries?

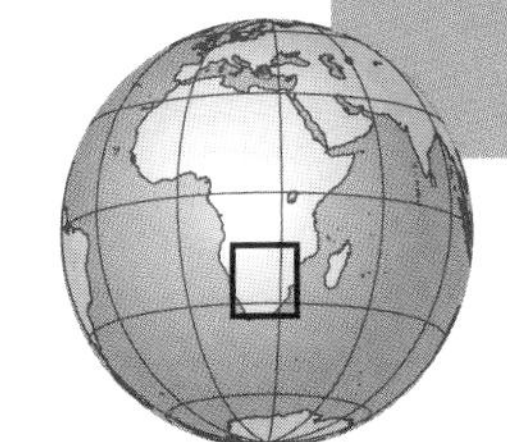

The Jewel of the Kalahari

Gabarone

Botswana was once one of the poorest countries in Africa. It used to be called Bechuanaland. After gaining independence from Great Britain in 1966, it was renamed Botswana. The new name came from that of the main group of people living there, the Tswana, or Batswana. In 1967 large **deposits** of diamonds were discovered in the region. Suddenly Botswana was one of Africa's richest countries.

Botswana is located in southern Africa. Its capital city is Gabarone. Most of the country's area is a dry region called the Kalahari. This is known as the sandveld, or 'thirstland'. The thirstland is different from a true desert because it has some grass and trees. In eastern Botswana there are rocky ranges of hills.

In the north-west is the Okavango River, which flows in from Namibia. It has been called 'the river that never finds the sea' because it ends in Botswana instead of flowing into the ocean. The place where it ends is called the Okavango **delta**. This huge swampy area has thick clumps of **papyrus** and much wildlife, including lions, hippopotamuses, and zebras. Many of the animals are protected in the Moremi Wildlife Reserve.

Botswana has forests in the north and east. Some of the trees produce fruits such as the marula or nuts such as the mongongo, which are important to the diet of the local people. Their diet also includes beans, meat, and **porridge** made with sorghum or maize. Some people eat dried caterpillars as a snack!

DID YOU KNOW?

The San people of the Kalahari speak an unusual language. It's called a 'click language' because it has many clicking sounds as parts of words. It is nearly impossible to speak that language if you don't learn it while you are growing up.

LEARN MORE! READ THESE ARTICLES…
DESERTS (VOLUME 1) • DIAMONDS (VOLUME 1)
SOUTH AFRICA: DIAMOND COUNTRY (VOLUME 8)

Many people in Botswana live in small towns and villages such as this one in the Okavango delta region of the country.

Answer: Diamonds were discovered in Botswana.

SEARCH LIGHT
Where did the first people to live in Madagascar come from?

Island Sanctuary

The Republic of Madagascar lies more than 400 kilometres off the south-eastern coast of Africa in the Indian Ocean. It occupies the fourth largest island in the world; only Greenland, New Guinea, and Borneo are larger. The capital of Madagascar is Antananarivo. It is located in the centre of the country.

Antananarivo

Even though Madagascar is so close to Africa, its people are not mainly African. The first people to live on the island were Malagasy people from Indonesia, almost 5,000 kilometres to the east. They arrived in about AD 700. People from Africa, Europe, and other parts of Southeast Asia came later. The people of Madagascar are still called Malagasy, but today their culture is a unique mix of Asian and African influences.

About half of the Malagasy follow Christianity. Most of the rest practise a traditional religion that has been passed down through the years. These people believe that the dead can reward or punish the living. They bury the dead in richly decorated tombs. They spend more time, money, and care on building tombs than they do on their houses.

For thousands of years Madagascar was covered with forests. But over time most of the trees have been cut down to make room for rice fields. The loss of the forests has been difficult for many of the animals of Madagascar - especially the lemurs. Lemurs look something like monkeys with long bushy tails. They are found in the wild only in Madagascar and on nearby islands. Madagascar also has many unique kinds of birds, chameleons, and butterflies. There are about 800 types of butterflies alone!

DID YOU KNOW?

The coelacanth, a fish thought to have been extinct for 60 million years, was found in the waters near Madagascar in the 1900s. Such animals are sometimes called 'living fossils' because their appearance and other physical traits have not changed for millions of years.

LEARN MORE! READ THESE ARTICLES...
BUTTERFLIES (VOLUME 11) • INDONESIA (VOLUME 7)
LEMURS (VOLUME 12)

Rice fields line a hillside in Madagascar.
© Chris Hellier/Corbis

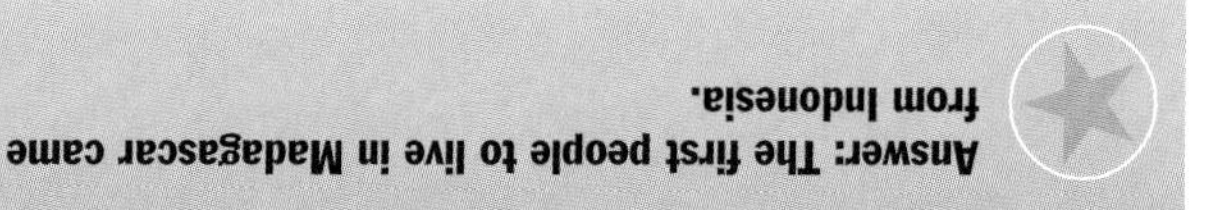

Fill in the gap: Lake Malawi is one of the world's _______ lakes.

Many homes are clustered along the shores of Lake Malawi, a large deep lake in eastern Malawi. It takes up nearly a fifth of Malawi's total area.
© Anthony Bannister—Gallo Images/Corbis

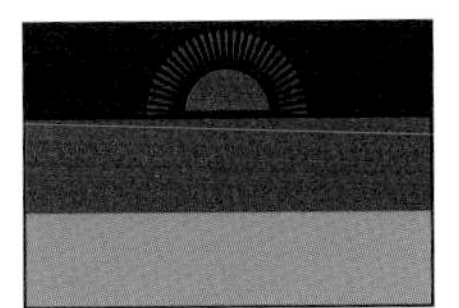

Malawi is a long, narrow country in southern Africa. Its capital is Lilongwe. The country's name comes from the Maravi, a Bantu-speaking group of people. They invaded the area and settled there about 600 years ago. When the British ruled Malawi, it was called Nyasaland. The name was changed to Malawi in 1964, when the country became independent.

The landscape of the country is made up of wide **plateaus**, deep valleys, and mountains. A large lake stretches along much of the eastern part of Malawi. The people who live in the country call it Lake Malawi, but people in other countries call it Lake Nyasa. It is one of the world's deepest lakes. There are about 200 kinds of fish in this lake. Many of these fish are not found anywhere else in the world.

There are many different kinds of plants and animals in Malawi. There are antelope, buffalo, elephants, leopards, lions, rhinoceroses, and zebras. These animals are found mostly in special parks. Much of the country is covered by grassy **savannahs**, but there are also forests and woodlands. Eucalyptus and pine trees have been planted to provide Malawi with wood and paper products.

Most of the people in Malawi today are farmers. They grow maize, beans, peas, and peanuts. There are big tea **plantations** as well. Tobacco is grown in the middle of the country. Malawi sells most of its tobacco to the United Kingdom. Tea, sugar, and cotton are also sold to other countries.

The flag of Malawi has three colours: black, red, and green. The black stands for the African people of Malawi. The red stands for the blood of those who died to make Malawi a free country. And the green stands for the natural beauty of the country.

Lilongwe

LEARN MORE! READ THESE ARTICLES…
EUCALYPTUS (VOLUME 10) • FISH (VOLUME 11)
LILONGWE, MALAWI (VOLUME 8)

SEARCH LIGHT
Find and correct the mistake in the following sentence: Lilongwe is where coffee, the country's main crop, is sold.

On Malawi's Fertile Plains

The capital of Malawi, a country in southern Africa, is Lilongwe. It is largely a planned city. It was not founded until 1947, when it was established as a trading centre. The city is in the central part of the country. In the late 1960s the leaders of Malawi decided to try to develop this central area of the country further. As part of their plan, they moved the capital from Zomba to Lilongwe in 1975.

DID YOU KNOW?

Although it is Malawi's capital, Lilongwe is only the second largest city in the country. Blantyre, in the south, is the largest city in Malawi and also the main centre of industry and commerce.

In addition to being a government centre, Lilongwe provides a market for local farmers to sell their crops. Some of the country's best farmland surrounds Lilongwe. This region produces tobacco, the main crop that Malawi sells to other countries. In Lilongwe you can visit the tobacco auction floors, where large amounts of tobacco are sold.

The city has two main sections, the old city and Capital Hill. The old city has the central market, cafés, and restaurants. People go there regularly to shop. The newer part of the city, on Capital Hill, has government buildings, hotels, and **embassies**. Between the two sections of the city is a nature sanctuary, which provides protection for the native animals and plants. The sanctuary covers about 148 hectares and is home to many different kinds of birds.

Because of its central location, many people travel through Lilongwe on their way to other parts of the country. The city has an international airport. It also has rail connections to Salima in the east and the Zambian border on the west.

LEARN MORE! READ THESE ARTICLES…
BIRDS (VOLUME 11) • HARARE, ZIMBABWE (VOLUME 8) • MALAWI (VOLUME 8)

Tobacco is sold at an auction in Lilongwe. The city is the centre of Malawi's tobacco processing and trading industries. Malawi is one of Africa's top tobacco producers.
David Else/Lonely Planet Images

Answer: Lilongwe is where tobacco, the country's main crop, is sold.

A Beautiful, Arid Place

Namibia is a country in south-western Africa. It is named for the Namib Desert, which covers much of the west side of the country. The desert is at least 80 million years old. It is huge and empty and is one of the most arid (driest) places on Earth.

Windhoek

Namibia is a young country. South Africa controlled Namibia until March 1990, when Namibia gained its independence. Windhoek, in the centre of the country, is Namibia's capital city. English is the official language of Namibia. But most of the people usually speak African languages.

Namibia's landscape is beautiful and varied. It has a coastline, deserts, mountains, and canyons. It is usually very dry and hot. In the summer it can get as hot as 49°C in the desert. Sometimes Namibia doesn't have any rain for long periods of time. Most of Namibia's rivers flow only after strong rains. But in the north-east there are tropical swamplands.

Namibia has plenty of wildlife. Etosha National Park is one of the largest parks for wild animals in the world. It is a popular attraction for **tourists**. Antelope, giraffes, impala, lions, leopards, rhinoceroses, and zebras can all be found in the park. It also has more than 600 bird species.

Mining is very important to Namibia's economy. Among the country's most valuable minerals are diamonds, copper, uranium, silver, and gold. But not many people are needed to work in mining. Even though much of the country is desert, more than a third of Namibians are farmers.

SEARCH LIGHT

Which of the following sentences is true?
a) All the land in Namibia is desert.
b) The Namib Desert is very old.
c) Most of Namibia gets plenty of rain.

LEARN MORE! READ THESE ARTICLES…
BIRDS (VOLUME 11) • DESERTS (VOLUME 1)
WINDHOEK, NAMIBIA (VOLUME 8)

Mountains and scattered trees break up the vast desert landscape in parts of Namibia.

DID YOU KNOW?

About 650,000 fur seals breed along the coast of Namibia every year. They'd better like the fog, because the coast is covered with fog about 160 days of the year.

Answer: b) The Namib Desert is very old.

DID YOU KNOW?

The country's first university, the University of Namibia, was founded in Windhoek in 1992.

Namibia's Windy Corner

SEARCH LIGHT

Among the area's first residents were
a) Germans and South Africans.
b) Aigams and Namib.
c) Herero and Khoekhoe.

Windhoek is the capital city of Namibia, a country in southern Africa. The city lies at a height of more than 1,654 metres. It is surrounded by a ring of hills. These hills protect it from the most violent of the dry winds blowing in from the Kalahari Desert to the east and the Namib Desert to the west. The city's name comes from a German word that means 'windy corner'. Windhoek is free of fiercely blowing winds for less than four months of the year.

The Herero and Khoekhoe peoples were among the first settlers in the region. Before the Europeans arrived, the city was called Aigams. This name means 'hot water' and referred to the **hot springs** in the area. Germany claimed the town for itself in 1890. South Africa took over the region, then known as South West Africa, 25 years later. When Namibia became independent in 1990, Windhoek was made the nation's capital.

Windhoek is also the country's chief economic centre. It sits in the middle of the grazing lands of the Karakul sheep. The skins of very young Karakul lambs are processed and transported by a number of furriers in Windhoek. This business employs many people in the city.

Herero women in traditional dress, Windhoek.

Windhoek has several interesting places and buildings to visit. The Alte Feste (Old Fort), built by the Germans, is one of the oldest buildings in the city. It is now a history museum. Christuskirche is an attractive church that was also built during German colonial times. And the city's St George's Cathedral is the smallest functional **cathedral** in southern Africa.

LEARN MORE! READ THESE ARTICLES…
GERMANY (VOLUME 6) • NAMIBIA (VOLUME 8) • SHEEP (VOLUME 12)

These buildings on a street in Windhoek display a mixture of styles, some modern and some from the time when Germany controlled the town.

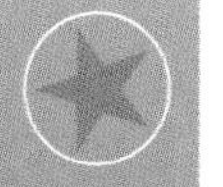

Answer: c) Herero and Khoekhoe.

Diamond Country

South Africa is the southernmost country on the African continent. The Atlantic Ocean and the Indian Ocean lie to its south. Johannesburg is the country's business centre and one of its largest cities. South Africa has three capital cities. Pretoria is the **administrative** centre, while Cape Town is where the **legislature** meets. The judicial capital, Bloemfontein, is the centre of the nation's court system.

South Africa is a beautiful country with many mountains. The tallest peaks are nearly 3,350 metres high. A large part of the country lies on a **tableland** called the Karoo. The rock formations of the Karoo are more than 200 million years old.

Because South Africa's climate is dry, people have to save water. The limited rainfall supports **savannahs** and, in higher areas, grasslands with few trees. The country has more than 20,000 kinds of flowering plants. But only scrub and scattered bush grow in the dry Karoo.

The country's many wild animals include lions, leopards, elephants, and rhinoceroses. There are also hippopotamuses, baboons, antelope, jackals, and buffalo. Many of these animals can be seen in Kruger National Park, a large nature preserve set up to protect wildlife.

Mining is a major industry in the country. Half of the world's known gold deposits are in South Africa. Diamonds and gold were discovered in the area in the late 1800s. South Africa later became wealthy by selling these products to other countries. It's the world's largest producer of the metals platinum, chromium, and gold.

LEARN MORE! READ THESE ARTICLES…
DIAMONDS (VOLUME 1) • SOUTH AFRICA: A PEOPLE APART (VOLUME 8)
SOUTH AFRICAN CITIES (VOLUME 8)

SEARCH LIGHT

True or false? Johannesburg is one of South Africa's capital cities.

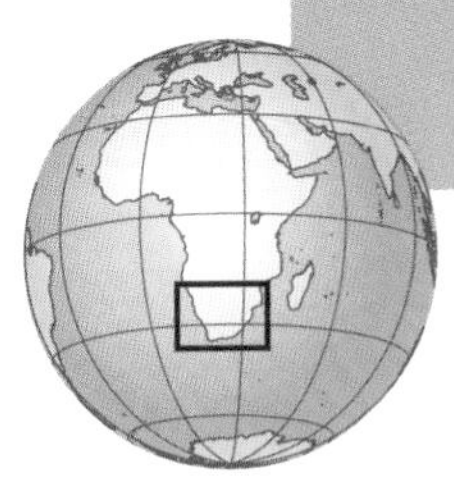

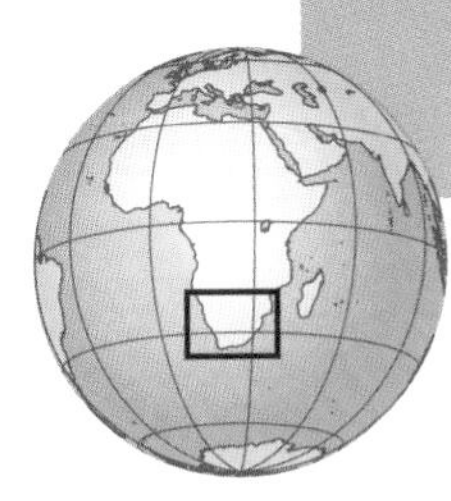

DID YOU KNOW?
In 1905 the world's largest gem diamond was found in what is now South Africa. The huge stone was cut into more than 100 jewels. The largest, the Great Star of Africa, is now part of the British crown jewels.

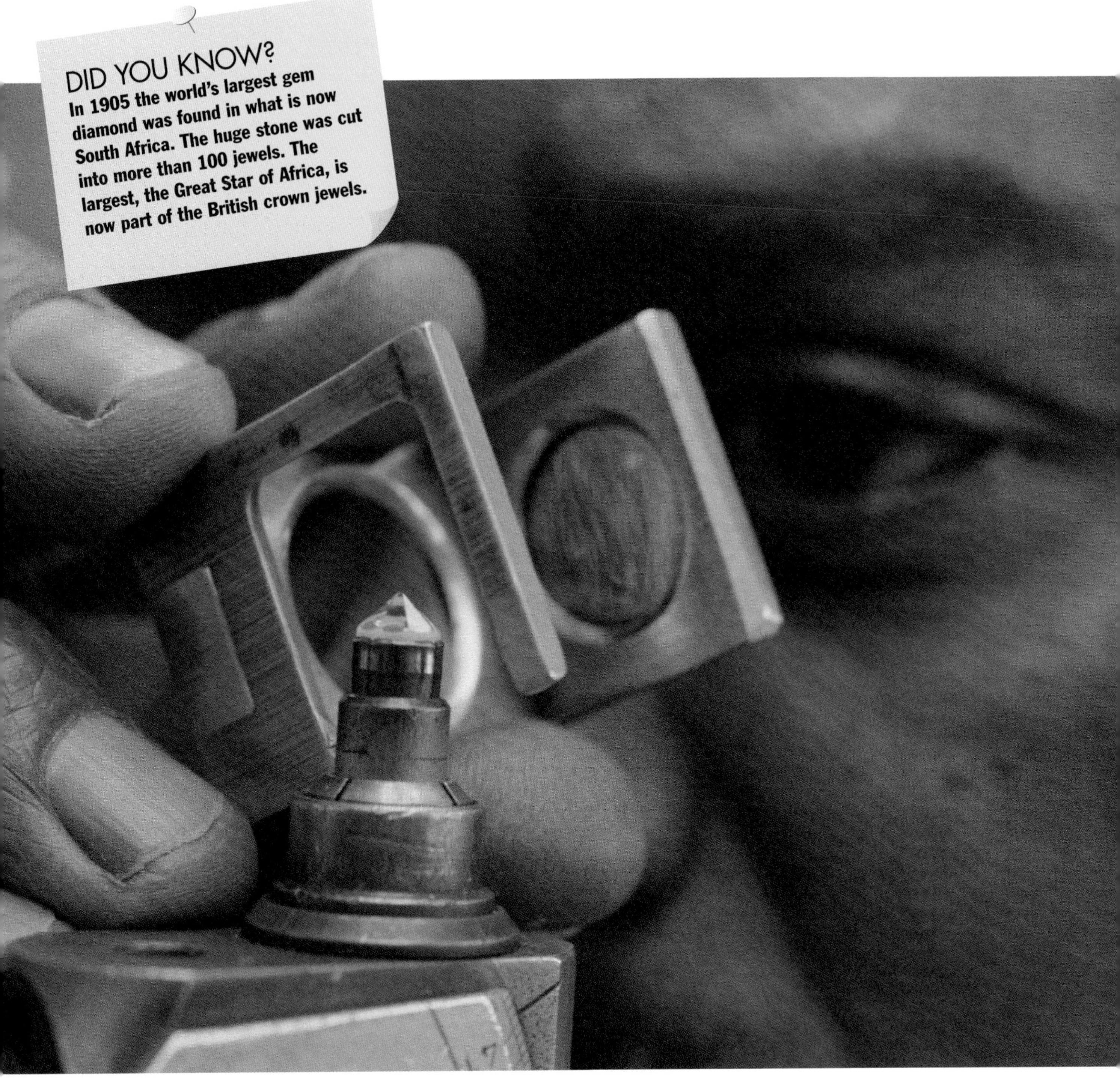

Diamond mining and cutting are major industries in South Africa. Here a diamond cutter in Johannesburg uses a lens to examine a partly cut diamond. Each cut must be carefully planned.

Answer: FALSE. Johannesburg is the country's business centre, but the three capitals are Pretoria, Cape Town, and Bloemfontein.

DID YOU KNOW?

Mahatma Gandhi led his first political protest in South Africa. Before Gandhi began fighting for India's independence from Britain, he lived for a time in South Africa. He helped the Indians who lived there fight for their rights.

A People Apart

SEARCH LIGHT

Find and correct the mistake in the following sentence: Under apartheid, most of South Africa's land was reserved for nonwhites.

For several hundred years, most of South Africa's people had few freedoms. There are four main groups of South Africans today: black Africans, white Africans, people whose families came from India, and people of mixed origins. The whites make up a fairly small number of the country's people. But for a long time they held all the power. Nonwhites had many of their basic rights taken away.

In the 1650s the Dutch set up the first permanent European settlement in South Africa. The British and Dutch fought for control over the area during the 1800s. In 1910 the British established the Union of South Africa. Black Africans, the **majority** of the population, were not allowed to vote or hold political office.

A restroom reserved for whites only during the time of apartheid in South Africa.
© Dave G. Houser/Corbis

In 1948 the government introduced a policy called apartheid. The word apartheid means 'apartness' in the Dutch language of Afrikaans. This policy gave most of the country's land to white people. Black Africans and other nonwhites were forced to live in separate areas and could enter areas where whites lived only if they had a pass. They had separate and worse schools and could hold only certain jobs. They could not vote or take part in government.

One of the leaders in the fight against apartheid was Nelson Mandela. Because of this, the government jailed him from 1962 to 1990. But black Africans continued to support Mandela. The country began to do away with apartheid in 1990. Mandela became South Africa's president in 1991, and he became a symbol of freedom throughout the world. The country's laws now support equal rights for everyone. But South Africa is still recovering from the effects of the many years of apartheid.

LEARN MORE! READ THESE ARTICLES…
LADYSMITH BLACK MAMBAZO (VOLUME 3) • NELSON MANDELA (VOLUME 4)
SOUTH AFRICA: DIAMOND COUNTRY (VOLUME 8)

President Nelson Mandela celebrates with a choir after signing South Africa's new constitution in December 1996. The constitution promised equal rights for all of the country's people.
© Charles O'Rear/Corbis

Answer: Under apartheid, most of South Africa's land was reserved for whites.

Table Mountain provides a scenic backdrop for Cape Town's fine harbour.
© Charles O'Rear/Corbis

DID YOU KNOW?
Johannesburg is the world's largest city that can't be reached by ships. It is located inland and has no major lakes or rivers. But the area's gold attracted many settlers there in the 1890s even though there was no port.

Mixed Urban Histories

Soweto was a town set aside for
a) Asians.
b) blacks.
c) whites.

Pretoria, the city of jacarandas, is one of the three capitals of South Africa. In the spring you see the purple blossoms of the jacaranda trees all along the city's streets.

Pretoria is a well-planned city. It was founded in 1855 by Marthinus, son of the Boer statesman Andries Pretorius. The Boers were farmers whose families moved from the Netherlands to settle in South Africa. Pretoria became the **administrative** capital of South Africa in 1910. The city boasts several museums, including the home of the famous Boer statesman Paul Kruger. Several monuments also celebrate the city's Boer past. Pretoria has many parks and the national zoo.

Near Pretoria is Johannesburg, one of South Africa's largest cities. Johannesburg was founded in 1886 after gold was discovered there. It is the country's business centre.

Just outside Johannesburg is Soweto. The city was developed under South Africa's former system of apartheid and was only for black people. Under apartheid, blacks and whites were kept separate. Blacks lived under very hard conditions and faced **discrimination**.

No visitor should leave South Africa without seeing Cape Town, near Africa's southern tip. It is known as one of the most beautiful cities in the world. In the oldest area of the city lies Table Mountain. It offers fantastic views of the city. It's also a very windy place and has its own cloud cover, called the Tablecloth. Cape Town is the **legislative** capital of South Africa. It is where the country's leaders make laws.

The country's highest court meets at Bloemfontein, the judicial capital of South Africa. The city's name means 'fountain of flowers', and it's known for its parks and gardens.

LEARN MORE! READ THESE ARTICLES…
THE NETHERLANDS (VOLUME 6) • SOUTH AFRICA: DIAMOND COUNTRY (VOLUME 8)
SOUTH AFRICA: A PEOPLE APART (VOLUME 8)

Answer: b) blacks.

DID YOU KNOW?

A musical instrument called the *mbira* has a long tradition among the Shona people of Zimbabwe. It has metal keys attached to a hand-sized board, and it's played with the thumbs and a forefinger. Westerners sometimes call it a 'thumb piano'.

From Colony to Independent Country

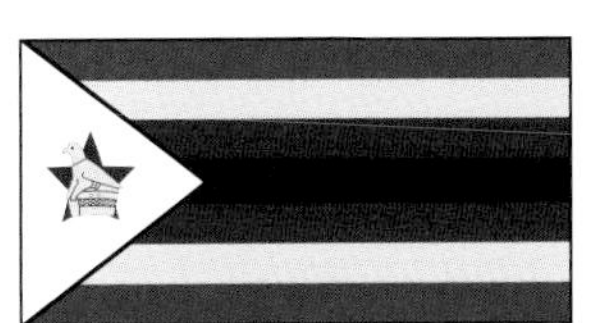

Zimbabwe is a country in southern Africa. For many years it was called Southern Rhodesia. It was named after Cecil Rhodes, who took control of the area for Great Britain. In the late 20th century, the country became fully independent and took the name Zimbabwe. The capital city is Harare.

Most Zimbabweans are black Africans of either the Shona or the Ndebele ethnic group. A small number of the people are white. Although most of the people speak either Shona or Ndebele, English is the official language.

The region spent many years under British colonial rule. In 1965 the small group of white people who ran the country declared it independent. But Britain refused to give up its rule. In 1980 Zimbabwe officially gained independence and **majority rule**. But the country continues to face many internal problems.

Two of Zimbabwe's most interesting geographic features are formed by the Zambezi River. This river flows along Zimbabwe's border with Zambia. At one point the entire river plunges over a steep cliff. This forms one of the world's mightiest waterfalls, Victoria Falls.

Also along this border is one of the world's largest artificial lakes, Lake Kariba. It was created when the huge Kariba Dam was built over the Zambezi River. About a third of Zimbabwe's electric power is generated from **water power** at this dam. Lake Kariba is also a popular fishing spot. Hippopotamuses and elephants live along its shores. And nearby lies the Hwange National Park, one of the last great elephant **sanctuaries** of Africa.

SEARCH LIGHT

Where does about a third of Zimbabwe's electricity come from? (Hint: Think 'water'.)

LEARN MORE! READ THESE ARTICLES...
ENGLAND (VOLUME 6) • HARARE, ZIMBABWE (VOLUME 8)
WATER POWER (VOLUME 2)

The Kariba Dam stretches across the Zambezi River. The statue in the foreground depicts the river god of the local people.
© Roger De La Harpe—Gallo Images/Corbis

Answer: Water power at the Kariba Dam is used to produce about a third of the country's electricity.

DID YOU KNOW?

Girls in Zimbabwe used to start wearing jewellery at a young age and never take it off. As they grew older, they would simply add more beads and bangles to their jewellery. Some women would end up wearing more than 20 kilos of jewellery.

City in a Garden

Harare is the capital of the African country of Zimbabwe. It lies on a broad high ridge called the Highveld in the country's north-eastern garden region. Harare is green with trees and bright with flowers.

Jacaranda trees line the streets of Harare.
Penny Tweedie/Panos Pictures

The city was founded in 1890. It was named Salisbury after Lord Salisbury, the British prime minister. As with much of southern Africa, Zimbabwe came under British rule in the late 1890s. The city developed only after 1899, when a railway line was established from the port of Beira in Mozambique to the east.

There were many industries that were started in Salisbury after World War II. People started moving into this city, and gradually the population grew. The city itself is modern and well planned, with high-rise buildings and tree-lined avenues.

In 1980 the new government of independent Zimbabwe renamed the city Harare. This honoured Chief Neharawe, who originally occupied this area with his people. The word Harare means 'one that does not sleep' in the Shona language.

Harare is still the centre of Zimbabwe's industry and **commerce**. It is the main place where crops from the surrounding farmlands are received and then distributed. There are also important gold mines nearby.

The University of Zimbabwe is located in Harare. The city is also home to the National Archives, which displays historical documents. At the National Gallery of Zimbabwe you can see an impressive collection of African painting and sculpture. And every year the city holds the Harare International Festival of the Arts. At this festival you can see all kinds of artistic performances, from traditional dancing and drumming to the plays of William Shakespeare.

SEARCH LIGHT

Harare is located on the
a) high seas.
b) Highveld.
c) highway.

LEARN MORE! READ THESE ARTICLES…
ENGLAND (VOLUME 6) • SCULPTURE (VOLUME 3) • ZIMBABWE (VOLUME 8)

Modern high-rise buildings loom over the city of Harare, Zimbabwe.
Richard I'Anson/Lonely Planet Images

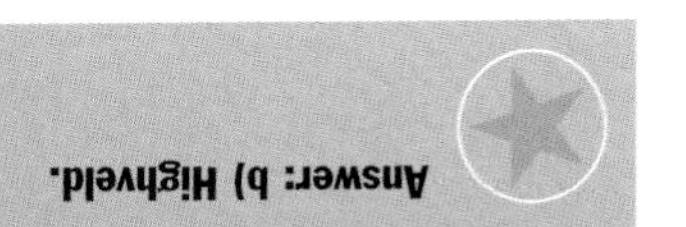

'The Smoke That Thunders'

It is difficult to stand in front of this spectacular African waterfall without feeling small. Victoria Falls is about twice as high as Niagara Falls in North America and about one and a half times as wide. It inspires awe and respect in all who see it.

Victoria Falls lies on the border between Zambia and Zimbabwe in southern Africa along the course of the Zambezi River.

The falls span the entire **breadth** of the Zambezi River at one of its broadest points. There is a constant roaring sound as the river falls. A dense blanket of mist covers the entire area. The Kalolo-Lozi people who live in the area call this mist Mosi-oa-Tunya, 'the Smoke That Thunders'.

The first European to set eyes on this wonder of nature was the British explorer David Livingstone. He named it after Queen Victoria.

The waters of Victoria Falls drop down a deep **gorge**. All the water of the Zambezi River flows in through this gorge. At the end of the gorge is the Boiling Pot, a deep pool into which the waters churn and foam during floods. The river waters then emerge into an enormous zigzag channel that forms the beginning of the Batoka Gorge.

The Victoria Falls Bridge is used for all traffic between Zambia and Zimbabwe. When it opened in 1905, it was the highest bridge in the world.

In 1989 Victoria Falls and its parklands were named a World Heritage site.

LEARN MORE! READ THESE ARTICLES…
NIAGARA FALLS (VOLUME 9) • RIVERS (VOLUME 1) • ZIMBABWE (VOLUME 8)

DID YOU KNOW?
Victoria Falls is huge, but another waterfall takes the record for being the tallest. Angel Falls in Venezuela dwarfs Victoria at an amazing 979 metres tall.

SEARCH LIGHT

The average height of Niagara Falls is about 50 metres. So what height would you estimate for Victoria Falls? (Hint: Look in the first paragraph.)

Answer: Victoria Falls is about twice as high as Niagara Falls. So you can estimate Victoria Falls at 100 metres.

GLOSSARY

administrative having to do with managing or supervising the functions of a business, organization, or government

Arab member of a people originating in the Arabian Peninsula and now inhabiting much of the Middle East and North Africa

archives place where public records or historical documents are kept

basin the area of land drained by a river and its branches

bay part of a coastline that curves in towards land

bazaar marketplace where many kinds of goods are sold; *especially*, such a marketplace in Asia or Africa

Berber member or descendant of a people who originally inhabited North Africa, before the Arab conquest in the 7th century AD

botanical (noun: botany) having to do with plant life

breadth width

canal artificial waterway for boats or for draining or supplying water to land

cassava tropical plant that has a thick underground root-like part and can be made into a number of foods

cathedral large church where a bishop is in charge

civil war war between opposing groups of citizens of the same country

civilization the way of life of a people at a particular time or place; also, a fairly advanced culture and technology

climate average weather in a particular area

colony (verb: colonize) settlement set up in a distant territory and controlled by a more powerful and expanding nation

commerce (adjective: commercial) the buying and selling of goods, especially on a large scale and between different places

delta large triangular area made of material deposited at the mouth of a river, where it empties into the sea

democracy (adjective: democratic) government in which the highest power is held by the citizens; they either use their power directly (usually by voting) or choose others to act for them

deposit substance laid down by a natural process

dialect one of several varieties of a language used by the members of a particular group or class of people

dictator person who rules with total power, often in a cruel or brutal way

discrimination the treatment of some individuals or groups differently from others without any fair or proper reason

diverse varied; different

drastic huge, extreme, or dramatic

dynasty series of rulers of the same family

economy the system in a country or group by which goods are made, services are offered, and both are sold and used

elevation the height of an object above sea level (that is, the surface of the ocean)

embassy the living quarters or office of an ambassador (a person who officially represents his or her own government in a foreign country)

endangered species a group of plants or animals whose entire survival is threatened

ethnic having to do with a large group of people who share a racial, national, tribal, religious, language, or cultural background

export to carry or send abroad, especially for sale in another country

extinct no longer existing

fertile rich and productive; able to yield quality crops in large quantities

fortify to strengthen with weapons and by military defences

gorge narrow steep-walled canyon

headquarters the governing and directing centre of an organization

heritage background or descent

highland high or mountainous land

hot spring a source of hot water coming from underground

inanimate not living

isthmus narrow strip of land connecting two larger land areas

legacy something handed down from an earlier time or person

legislature organized government group with the power to make laws

majority most; usually, more than half of a group of individual people or things

majority rule system in which the majority (that is, a number over half) of a group is given the power to make decisions that the entire group must accept

mammal class of warm-blooded animals that feed their young with milk from special mammary glands, have an internal backbone, and are more or less covered with hair

mangrove tropical tree or shrub that has partly exposed roots and grows in thickly in areas of salty water

manufacture to make from raw materials, by hand or by machine

meditation (verb: meditate) a quiet focussed concentration, meant to calm and clear the mind; sometimes used to reach a spiritual awareness

mosque Muslim place of worship

network complex system

nomad member of a people who have no permanent home but instead move from place to place, usually with the seasons and within a specific area

papyrus tall reed plant that grows in the Nile valley and that the ancient Egyptians used to make an early kind of paper

petroleum liquid taken from the ground and not yet cleaned or separated into such products as petrol and paraffin; also called crude oil

pilgrim person who travels to a shrine or holy place to worship

plantation large farming property, usually worked by resident labourers

plateau wide land area with a fairly level surface raised sharply above the land on at least one side

porridge soft food made by boiling grain meal or a vegetable in milk or water until it thickens

poverty the condition of being poor

prophet holy person who acts as a messenger between God and people; also, a gifted person with the ability to correctly predict future events

rainforest dense tropical woodland with a high yearly rainfall and very tall trees

republic form of government in which the leader is not a monarch and is usually a president

reserve area of land set apart for some special purpose; also (usually plural, *reserves*), money or valuable items kept in hand or set apart until needed

sanctuary safe place

savannah hot dry grassland with scattered trees

seaport port, harbour, or town reachable by seagoing ships

shrine place where honour or worship is offered to a saint or deity

splendour something very grand or beautiful

sultan king or ruler, especially of a Muslim state

tableland broad flat area of high land

tamarind tropical tree whose sharp-tasting fruit is used as a flavouring

teeming crowded

tomb special building or room in which a dead person is buried

tourism business of encouraging travel to a specific location and of managing services for visitors (including lodging, transport, food, and activities)

tourist person who travels for pleasure

tropical having to do with the Earth's warmest and most humid (moist) climates

truce temporary stop in fighting during a war or other violent conflict

vast huge or spacious

water power energy produced by moving water that can be used to do physical work; it may come directly from water's own force or from machines run by water that in turn produce even greater power (such as electricity)